# Modernizing Enterprise Java
*A Concise Cloud Native Guide for Developers*

*Markus Eisele and Natale Vinto*

Beijing · Boston · Farnham · Sebastopol · Tokyo

**Modernizing Enterprise Java**

by Markus Eisele and Natale Vinto

Copyright © 2022 Markus Eisele and Natale Vinto. All rights reserved.

Published by O'Reilly Media, Inc., 1005 Gravenstein Highway North, Sebastopol, CA 95472.

O'Reilly books may be purchased for educational, business, or sales promotional use. Online editions are also available for most titles (*http://oreilly.com*). For more information, contact our corporate/institutional sales department: 800-998-9938 or *corporate@oreilly.com*.

| | |
|---|---|
| **Acquisitions Editor:** Suzanne McQuade | **Indexer:** nSight, Inc. |
| **Development Editors:** Nicole Taché, Amelia Blevins | **Interior Designer:** David Futato |
| **Production Editor:** Caitlin Ghegan | **Cover Designer:** Karen Montgomery |
| **Copyeditor:** Piper Editorial Consulting, LLC | **Illustrator:** Kate Dullea |
| **Proofreader:** Pider Editorial Consulting, LLC | |

November 2021:     First Edition

**Revision History for the First Edition**

2021-10-20:    First Release

See *https://oreil.ly/W0Bne* for release details.

The O'Reilly logo is a registered trademark of O'Reilly Media, Inc. *Modernizing Enterprise Java*, the cover image, and related trade dress are trademarks of O'Reilly Media, Inc.

The views expressed in this work are those of the authors, and do not represent the publisher's views. While the publisher and the authors have used good faith efforts to ensure that the information and instructions contained in this work are accurate, the publisher and the authors disclaim all responsibility for errors or omissions, including without limitation responsibility for damages resulting from the use of or reliance on this work. Use of the information and instructions contained in this work is at your own risk. If any code samples or other technology this work contains or describes is subject to open source licenses or the intellectual property rights of others, it is your responsibility to ensure that your use thereof complies with such licenses and/or rights.

This work is part of a collaboration between O'Reilly and Red Hat. See our statement of editorial independence (*https://oreil.ly/editorial-independence*).

978-1-098-10214-2

[LSI]

*To my family. None of this would be possible without them.*
*—Markus*

*To Fabrizio Scarcello, modernizer, innovator, dear friend.*
*—Natale*

# Table of Contents

# From Platform to Ecosystem

Unless you've been in deep seclusion for the past few years, you can't have missed the fact that the enterprise world has been moving toward adopting cloud technologies. This includes approaches such as microservices, Kubernetes, Linux containers, and so much more. However, despite the fact that Java has been the mainstay of enterprise developers for over two decades, it hasn't been immediately obvious that it has such a significant role in this new cloud world.

Java and the frameworks and stacks built with it are often viewed as monolithic, and slow to start, consuming a lot of memory or disk space, and the dynamic nature of Java itself seems to fly in the face of Kubernetes's immutability assumptions. For the many millions of Java developers out there, this could pose a serious problem, especially if we need to try to re-create in another language the richness of the Java ecosystem of IDEs, third party libraries, etc., which have helped to make developers so incredibly productive over the years.

Fortunately, the Java community of developers and vendors has met the challenge of cloud native Java head on. Changes in the Java language, frameworks, etc. have been made and adopted quickly, allowing Java developers to bring their skills to this new frontier. These include technologies such as Quarkus, GraalVM, Eclipse Vert.x, Spring Boot, and OpenJDK.

However, using them efficiently within a cloud environment is not always obvious. Where does CI/CD come into play? What about Linux container images and Kubernetes? Monitoring, observability, health checking of your microservices, and so much more can appear to be a daunting challenge, even for the most experienced developer.

Fortunately, in this book, Markus and Natale have provided the answers. Within these pages, you'll be taken through a journey of understanding and appreciation of what's happening within the Java world to better embrace cloud and also those technologies within the cloud that may not be familiar and yet are important to ensure your distributed microservices function well. Whether you're an experienced Java developer or a relative novice, this book is a great starting point for your journey into the cloud and beyond!

*— Mark Little*
*Vice President, Middleware Engineering, Red Hat*

# Preface

We wrote this book for developers who are looking to bring their monolithic, Java-based models successfully into the future. The roadmap for the book is as follows:

- Chapter 1 presents the fundamental technologies and concepts we will use throughout the book.

- Chapter 2 walks you through a complete microservices-based architecture implementation, using different Java frameworks for different components. We'll give an overview on how to split the typical monolithic approach into a more diverse and heterogeneous environment.

- Chapter 3 presents some basic migration strategies and shows you an evaluation path for the target development platform.

- Chapter 4 discusses how Java developers can benefit from Kubernetes capabilities to modernize and enhance their apps.

- Chapter 5 explores proven patterns, standardized tools, and open source resources that will help you create long-lasting systems that can grow and change with your needs.

- Chapter 6 demonstrates essential tasks in Kubernetes, such as logging, monitoring, and debugging apps.

- Chapter 7 analyzes how Java developers can create modern applications following a serverless execution model. We outlined some of the most common use cases and architectures that Java developers are likely to work with today and tomorrow.

# Conventions Used in This Book

The following typographical conventions are used in this book:

*Italic*
: Indicates new terms, URLs, email addresses, filenames, and file extensions.

`Constant width`
: Used for program listings, as well as within paragraphs to refer to program elements such as variable or function names, databases, data types, environment variables, statements, and keywords.

**`Constant width bold`**
: Shows commands or other text that should be typed literally by the user.

*`Constant width italic`*
: Shows text that should be replaced with user-supplied values or by values determined by context.

This element signifies a tip or suggestion.

This element signifies a general note.

This element indicates a warning or caution.

# Using Code Examples

Supplemental material (code examples, exercises, etc.) is available for download at *https://oreil.ly/modernentjava*.

If you have a technical question or a problem using the code examples, please send email to *bookquestions@oreilly.com*.

This book is here to help you get your job done. In general, if example code is offered with this book, you may use it in your programs and documentation. You do not need to contact us for permission unless you're reproducing a significant portion of the code. For example, writing a program that uses several chunks of code from this book does not require permission. Selling or distributing examples from O'Reilly books does require permission. Answering a question by citing this book and quoting example code does not require permission. Incorporating a significant amount of example code from this book into your product's documentation does require permission.

We appreciate, but generally do not require, attribution. An attribution usually includes the title, author, publisher, and ISBN. For example: "*Modernizing Enterprise Java* by Markus Eisele and Natale Vinto (O'Reilly). Copyright 2022 Markus Eisele and Natale Vinto, 978-1-098-10214-2."

If you feel your use of code examples falls outside fair use or the permission given above, feel free to contact us at *permissions@oreilly.com*.

## O'Reilly Online Learning

 For more than 40 years, *O'Reilly Media* has provided technology and business training, knowledge, and insight to help companies succeed.

Our unique network of experts and innovators share their knowledge and expertise through books, articles, and our online learning platform. O'Reilly's online learning platform gives you on-demand access to live training courses, in-depth learning paths, interactive coding environments, and a vast collection of text and video from O'Reilly and 200+ other publishers. For more information, visit *http://oreilly.com*.

## How to Contact Us

Please address comments and questions concerning this book to the publisher:

O'Reilly Media, Inc.
1005 Gravenstein Highway North
Sebastopol, CA 95472
800-998-9938 (in the United States or Canada)
707-829-0515 (international or local)
707-829-0104 (fax)

We have a web page for this book, where we list errata, examples, and any additional information. You can access this page at *https://oreil.ly/ModernJava*.

Email *bookquestions@oreilly.com* to comment or ask technical questions about this book.

For news and information about our books and courses, visit *http://oreilly.com*.

Find us on Facebook: *http://facebook.com/oreilly*.

Follow us on Twitter: *http://twitter.com/oreillymedia*.

Watch us on YouTube: *http://youtube.com/oreillymedia*.

# Acknowledgments

We both want to thank Jason "Jay" Dobies for his wild passion for getting through our German/Italian English. He not only helped us to be better writers but also gave valuable insight as an early reader. Thank you for having been part of this journey. Everybody says writing a book isn't easy. We did know that before we started. What we bluntly underestimated was the fact that we started writing at the beginning of a pandemic. We both went through more ups and downs than expected, and it is only because of our families and friends that we even got an opportunity to finish this book. We also can't praise the O'Reilly team enough for their patience, flexible deadlines, and open ears when we needed them. Thank you, Suzanne McQuade, Nicole Taché, and Amelia Blevins! Thank you, Red Hat. For providing an amazing place to work, learn, and grow. We love open source and sharing knowledge as much as probably everybody else in this company. To the many "Hatters" for their support on the way! Technical reviewers catch you at your weakest. Whenever we tried to sneak a little detail by them, they found it and asked the right questions. Thank you all for your dedication and inspirations along the way: Sébastien Blanc, Alex Soto, and Marc Hildenbrand! The heart of this book is not only the combined experience accumulated by us but first and foremost an example. This example was initialy created by Madou Coulibaly and Alex Groom. They used this to teach many developers how to effectivly build cloud native applications and allowed us to use their consise example as the base. #stayHealthy #wearAMask #protectYourLovedOnes

# CHAPTER 1

# Revisiting Enterprise Development

Enterprise development has always been one of the most exciting fields of software engineering, and the last decade has been a particularly fascinating period. The 2010s saw highly distributed microservices gradually replace classic three-tier architectures, with the almost limitless resources of cloud-based infrastructure pushing heavyweight application servers toward obsolescence. While developers are challenged with putting the pieces of the distributed world back together, plenty of voices question the necessity for this complex microservices world. The reality is that most applications are still well-crafted monolithic applications that follow a traditional software development process.

However, the way we deploy and operate software has changed equally fast. We have seen DevOps growing into GitOps, expanding developers' responsibilities beyond the application code including the required infrastructure. Building on Markus's book *Modern Java EE Design Patterns* (O'Reilly) (*https://oreil.ly/1cROz*), this book puts more perspective on modernization than just modularization. We want to help you understand the various pieces that lead to a modern Kubernetes-native development platform and how to build and maintain applications on top of it.

This book aims to step back and evaluate the success factors and drivers for application modernization and cloud native architectures. We focus on modernizing Java-based Enterprise Applications, including a selection process for which applications are suitable for modernization and an overview of tools and methodologies that help you manage your modernization efforts. Instead of talking about patterns, this book provides a set of examples to help you apply everything you've learned.

That said, this book isn't discussing monolithic versus distributed applications extensively. Rather, our goal is to help you understand how to seamlessly move your applications to the cloud.

You can use this book as a reference and read chapters in any order. We have organized the material, though, starting with higher-level concepts to implementation in iterations. First, it's important to start by looking at the different definitions of clouds and how we build applications for them.

## From Public to Private. Why Clouds?

The differences between public clouds, private clouds, hybrid clouds, and multiclouds were once easily defined by location and ownership. Today, these two are no longer the only relevant drivers for the classification of clouds. Let's start with a more comprehensive definition of the different target environments and why they are used.

A public cloud environment is usually created from resources not owned by the end user that can be redistributed to other tenants. Private cloud environments solely dedicate their resources to the end user, usually within the user's firewall, data center, or sometimes on premises. Multiple cloud environments with some degree of workload portability, orchestration, and management are called hybrid clouds. Decoupled, independent, and not connected clouds are commonly referred to as multiclouds. Hybrid and multicloud approaches are mutually exclusive; you can't have both simultaneously because the clouds will either be interconnected (hybrid cloud) or not (multicloud).

Deploying applications to a cloud, regardless of the type of cloud, is becoming more common across enterprises as they seek to improve security and performance through an expanded portfolio of environments. But security and performance are only two of many reasons to move workloads into hybrid or multicloud environments. The primary motivation for many is the pay-for-what-you-use model. Instead of investing in costly on-premises hardware that is hard and expensive to scale out, clouds offer resources when you need them. You don't have to invest in facilities, utilities, or building out your own data center. You do not even need dedicated IT teams to handle your cloud data center operations, as you can enjoy the expertise of your cloud provider's staff.

For developers, the cloud is about self-service and flexibility. You don't have to wait for environments to be promoted, and you can choose infrastructure components (e.g., databases, message brokers, etc.) as the need arises to free you from unnecessary wait times and ultimately speed up development cycles. Beyond these primary advantages, you can also find custom features for developers in some cloud environments. OpenShift, for example, has an integrated development console that provides developers with direct edit access to all details of their application topology. Cloud-based IDEs (e.g., Eclipse Che (*https://www.eclipse.org/che*)) provide browser-based access to development workspaces and eliminate local environment configuration for teams.

Additionally, cloud infrastructures encourage you to automate your deployment processes. Deployment automation enables you to deploy your software to testing and production environments with the push of a button—a mandatory requirement for Agile development and DevOps teams. You've seen a need for 100% automation already when you've read about microservices architectures. But automation goes well beyond the application parts. It extends to the infrastructure and downstream systems. Ansible (*https://www.ansible.com*), Helm (*https://helm.sh*), and Kubernetes Operators (*https://oreil.ly/lhaPm*) help you. We talk more about automation in Chapter 4, and you'll use an Operator in Chapter 7.

# What "Cloud Native" Means

You've probably heard of the *cloud native* approach for developing applications and services, and even more so since the Cloud Native Computing Foundation (CNCF) was founded in 2015 and released Kubernetes v1. Bill Wilder first used the term "cloud native" in his book, *Cloud Architecture Patterns* (O'Reilly) (*https://oreil.ly/ hmeAC*). According to Wilder, a cloud native application is architected to take full advantage of cloud platforms by using cloud platform services and scaling automatically. Wilder wrote his book during a period of growing interest in developing and deploying cloud native applications. Developers had various public and private platforms to choose from, including Amazon AWS, Google Cloud, Microsoft Azure, and many smaller cloud providers. But hybrid-cloud deployments were also becoming more prevalent around then, which presented challenges.

The CNCF (*https://oreil.ly/Sadph*) defines "cloud native" as:

> cloud native technologies empower organizations to build and run scalable applications in modern, dynamic environments such as public, private, and hybrid clouds. Containers, service meshes, microservices, immutable infrastructure, and declarative APIs exemplify this approach.
>
> These techniques enable loosely coupled systems that are resilient, manageable, and observable. Combined with robust automation, they allow engineers to make high-impact changes frequently and predictably with minimal toil.
>
> —CNCF Cloud Native Definition v1.0

Similar to cloud native technologies are the Twelve-Factor Apps (*https://12factor.net*). The Twelve-Factor Apps manifesto defines patterns for building applications that are delivered on the cloud. While these patterns overlap with Wilder's cloud architecture patterns, the Twelve-Factor methodology can be applied to apps written in any programming language and use any combination of backing services (database, queue, memory cache, etc.).

# Kubernetes-Native Development

For developers deploying applications to a hybrid cloud, shifting focus from cloud native to Kubernetes-native makes sense. One of the first mentions of "Kubernetes-native" is found as early as 2017. A blog post on Medium describes the differences between Kubernetes-native (*https://oreil.ly/2quU8*) and cloud native as a set of technologies that are optimized for Kubernetes. The key takeaway is that Kubernetes-native is a specialization of cloud native and not separated from what cloud native defines. Whereas a cloud native application is intended for the cloud, a Kubernetes-native application is designed and built for Kubernetes.

In the early days of cloud native development, orchestration differences prevented applications from being genuinely cloud native. Kubernetes resolves the orchestration problem, but Kubernetes does not cover cloud provider services (for example, Roles and Permissions) or provide an event bus (for example, Kafka). The idea that Kubernetes-native is a specialization of cloud native means that there are many similarities between them. The main difference is cloud provider portability. Taking full advantage of the hybrid cloud and using multiple cloud providers requires that applications are deployable to any cloud provider. Without such a feature, you're tied into a single cloud provider and reliant on them being up 100% of the time. To fully use the benefits of a hybrid cloud, applications have to be build in a Kubernetes-native way. Kubernetes-native is the solution to cloud portability concerns. We talk more about Kubernetes-native in Chapter 2.

# Containers and Orchestration for Developers

One key ingredient for portability is the *container*. A container represents a fraction of the host system resources together with the application. The origins of containers go back to early Linux days with the introduction of chroots, and they became mainstream with Google's process containers, which eventually became cgroups. Their use exploded in 2013 primarily because of Docker, which made them accessible for many developers. There is a difference between Docker the company, Docker containers, Docker images, and the Docker developer tooling we're all used to. While everything started with Docker containers, Kubernetes prefers to run containers through any container runtime (e.g. containerd (*https://containerd.io*) or CRI-O (*https://cri-o.io*)) that supports its Container Runtime Interface (CRI). What many people refer to as Docker images are actually images packaged in the Open Container Initiative (OCI) format (*https://opencontainers.org*).

## Container-Native Runtime

Containers offer a lighter-weight version of the Linux operating system's userland stripped down to the bare essentials. However, it's still an operating system, and the quality of a container matters just as much as the host operating system. It takes a lot of engineering, security analysis, and resources to support container images. It requires testing not just the base images but also their behavior on a given container host. Relying on certified and OCI-compliant base images removes hurdles when moving applications across platforms. Ideally, these base images already come with the necessary language runtimes you need. For Java-based applications, the Red Hat Universal Base Image (*https://oreil.ly/KH9od*) is a good starting point. We'll learn more about containers and how developers use them in Chapter 4.

## Kubernetes Flavors

We've talked about Kubernetes as a general concept so far. And we continue to use the word *Kubernetes* to talk about the technology that powers container orchestration. The name Kubernetes (or sometimes just K8s) refers to the open source project (*https://kubernetes.io*) that is widely understood to be the standards body for the core functionality of container orchestration. We use the term "plain" Kubernetes throughout the book if we refer to standard functionality inside Kubernetes. The Kubernetes community created different distributions and even flavors of Kubernetes. The CNCF runs the Certified Kubernetes Conformance Program (*https://oreil.ly/n4XH9*), which lists over 138 products from 108 vendors at the time of writing. The list contains complete distributions (e.g., MicroK8s, OpenShift, Rancher), hosted offerings (e.g., Google Kubernetes Engine, Amazon Elastic Kubernetes Service, Azure AKS Engine), and installers (e.g., minikube, VanillaStack). They all share the common core but add additional functionality or integrations on top as the vendors see a need or opportunity. We don't make any suggestions about which Kubernetes flavor to use in this book. You will have to decide on your own which direction you want to take your production workloads. To help you run the examples in this book locally, we use minikube (*https://oreil.ly/sCQUo*) and do not require you to have a full-blown installation somewhere in a cloud.

## Managing Development Complexity

One of the most critical areas of Kubernetes-native development is the management of your development environment. The number of tasks that need to be executed for a successful deployment or staging into multiple environments has grown exponentially. One reason is the growing number of individual application parts or microservices. Another reason is the application-specific configuration of necessary infrastructure. Figure 1-1 gives a brief overview of an example development environment with tools necessary for a fully automated development. We will talk about a fraction of them in this book to give you an easy start in your new environment. The core development tasks haven't changed. You will still write an application or service with a suitable framework, like Quarkus (*http://quarkus.io*), as we do in this book.

This part of the developer workflow is commonly referred to as "inner loop" development.

We will spend most of our time in this book walking through changes and opportunities in the "outer loop." The outer loop takes your built and tested application and puts it into production through various mechanisms. It is essential to understand that we are expressing some very strong opinions in this book. They reflect what we have learned about making Java developers productive, fast, and maybe even happy by using the tools and techniques we are recommending. As indicated in Figure 1-1, you have one or two choices to make in some places. We chose the more traditional way for Java developers in this book. We use Maven instead of Gradle for the application build and podman over Docker to build the container images. We also use the OpenJDK and not GraalVM and stick with JUnit instead of Testcontainers (*https:// oreil.ly/kbudT*) in the examples.

But the cloud native ecosystem, as mapped out by the CNCF landscape (*https:// oreil.ly/kqsG9*), has even more tools for you to choose from. Think of this book as a trail map for the Enterprise Java developer.

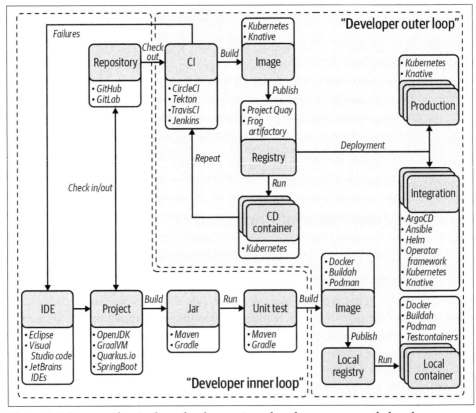

*Figure 1-1. Inner and outer loop development, and author-recommended tools*

Besides the technology choices, you'll also have to decide how you want to use this new ecosystem. With the variety of tools available comes another dimension that lets you choose your level of engagement with Kubernetes. We differentiate between opinionated and flexible as outlined in Figure 1-2. As a developer obsessed with details, you might want to learn all of the examples from the trenches and use plain Kubernetes while crafting your YAML files.

 Originally, YAML was said to mean Yet Another Markup Language. This name was intended as a tongue-in-cheek reference to its purpose as a markup language. But it was later repurposed as YAML Ain't Markup Language, a recursive acronym, to distinguish its purpose as data-oriented.

You may decide to focus exclusively on source code and don't want distraction from implementing business logic. This can be achieved with developer tools provided by some distributions. Depending on what's most important to you in your development process, there are various options. You can use the main Kubernetes command-line interface (CLI) kubectl instead of a product-specific one like OpenShift's CLI oc. If you want to be closer to a complete product, we suggest you try CodeReady Containers (*https://oreil.ly/vhyZ7*). It is an OpenShift cluster on your laptop with an easy getting started experience. But, the choice is yours.

Another great tool we would recommend is odo (*https://oreil.ly/IyjTm*), which is a general-purpose developer CLI for Kubernetes based projects. Existing tools such as kubectl and oc are more operations-focused and require a deep understanding of underlying concepts. Odo abstracts away complex Kubernetes concepts for the developer. Two example choices from the outer development loop are Continous Integration (CI) solutions. We use Tekton (*https://tekton.dev*) in this book, and you can use it in Chapter 6. It is also possible to use Jenkins on Kubernetes with the Jenkins Operator (*https://oreil.ly/0Z1Cv*) or even Jenkins X. Whatever choice you make, you will be the master of your Kubernetes-native journey after all.

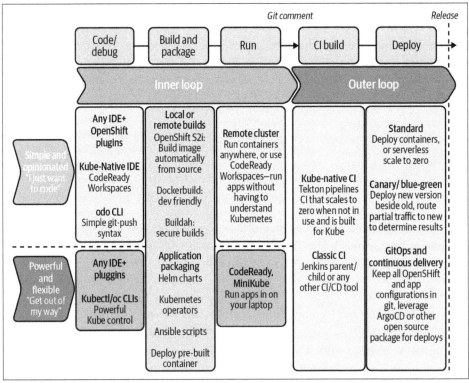

*Figure 1-2. Opinionated versus flexible—technology choices in inner and outer development loops*

# DevOps and Agility

When modernizing your Enterprise Java application, the next critical change is in the creation of cross-functional teams that share responsibilities from idea to operation. While some say that DevOps is solely focused on the operational aspects and paired with self-service for developers, we firmly believe that DevOps is a team culture focused on long-lasting impact. The word "DevOps" is a mashup of "development" and "operations," but it represents a set of ideas and practices much more significant than simply the sum of both terms. DevOps includes security, collaborative ways of working, data analytics, and many other things. DevOps describes approaches to speeding up the processes by which a new business requirement goes from code in development to deployment in a production environment. These approaches require that development teams and operations teams communicate frequently and work with empathy for their teammates. Scalability and flexible provisioning are also necessary. Developers, usually coding in a familiar development environment, work closely with IT operations to speed software builds, tests, and releases without sacrificing reliability. All this together results in more frequent code changes and more dynamic infrastructure usage. Changing a traditional IT organization from a traditional approach to a DevOps methodology is often described as *transformation* and is way beyond the scope of this book. Nevertheless, it is an essential ingredient, and you will see this transformation is beautifully described as "teaching elephants to dance" in books, articles, and presentations.

## Summary

In this chapter, you learned some basic definitions and heard about the most important technologies and concepts we are going to use throughout this book. The next chapter takes you into the source code of your first application modernization.

# CHAPTER 2

# The Path to Cloud Native Java

"Πάντα ῥεῖ" (Panta rei) is a famous aphorism from philosopher Heraclitus that describes the mutable condition of our existence where everything flows, where our call is to react and adapt. This perfectly describes the right approach to the evolution we are experiencing in the IT world in general, and specifically with programming languages and frameworks, where heterogeneous, distributed, multicloud workloads are more common and essential for business purposes.

Java and Jakarta EE (formely known as Java EE), are evolving as well in that direction, balancing the benefits that come from the consolidated experience of enterprise solutions, together with the need for a fast-changing cloud-aware scenario where our applications can run in many clouds seamlessly. In this chapter, we will outline the components needed for a transition to cloud native Java, walking you through an ecommerce store Java implementation called Coolstore.

## Cloud Native Workshop

Microservices are an accepted and well-recognized practice nowadays. For JavaEE developers, this means a lift-and-shift change of the paradigm, where a single application server does not contain all our business logic. Instead, it gets split into different microservices running in their application servers, like Tomcat or Undertow, with a minimal footprint and optimizations to keep this coexistence functional and performant also in the cloud native world.

The monolithic approach today can be refactored into a heterogeneous and even programming language agnostic model, where each module is managed by a specific component running in a different application. Beyond the best practices such as API-driven models, the challenge here is how to maintain this diversity. However, Java today provides a set of tools and frameworks that help us focus on our preferred tools and collaborate easily. In this chapter, you will learn how to develop and deploy a microservices-based application split across different Java frameworks.

# Architecture

Our ecommerce application Coolstore is a typical web app containing three components:

*Presentation layer*
   a frontend to show available items to acquire

*Model layer*
   a backend providing the business logic to catalog and index all items to sell

*Data layer*
   a database storing all records about transactions and items

The outcome of these components is an online store with a catalog of product items and an inventory of stock that we can organize with the architecture shown in Figure 2-1.

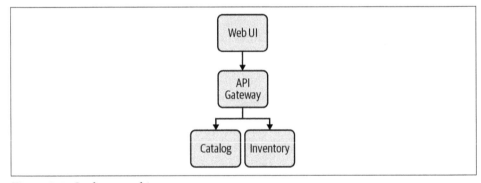

*Figure 2-1. Coolstore architecture*

We map the three previously mentioned components into several microservices, each one responsible for its layer:

- *Catalog Service* uses a REST API to expose the content of a catalog stored in a relational database.
- *Inventory Service* uses a REST API to expose the inventory of items stored in a relational database.
- *Gateway Service* calls the *Catalog Service* and *Inventory Service* in an efficient way.
- *WebUI Service* calls *Gateway Service* to retrieve all the information.

The Presentation and the Model layers are represented by such microservices, with the latter having an interface to the Data layer delegated to some DBMS. Our estore implementation is called Coolstore and looks like the picture in Figure 2-2.

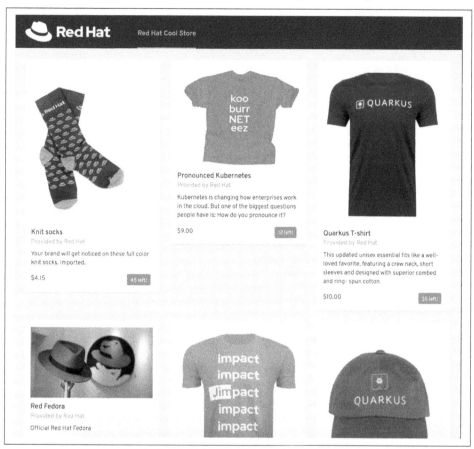

*Figure 2-2. Coolstore dashboard*

# Create an Inventory Microservice with Quarkus

Quarkus (*https://quarkus.io*) is a full stack, Kubernetes-native Java framework made for Java virtual machines (JVMs) and native compilation, optimizing Java specifically for containers and enabling it to become an effective platform for serverless, cloud, and Kubernetes environments.

It is designed to work with popular Java standards, frameworks, and libraries like Eclipse MicroProfile and Spring, as well as Apache Kafka, RESTEasy (JAX-RS), Hibernate ORM (JPA), Infinispan, Camel, and many more. It also provides the correct information to GraalVM (a universal virtual machine for running apps written in several languages, including Java and JavaScript) for a native compilation of your application.

Quarkus is a good choice for implementing microservices architectures, and it provides a set of tools that help developers debug and test at ease. For our ecommerce store, we will start using Quarkus for the Inventory microservice (as shown in Figure 2-3).

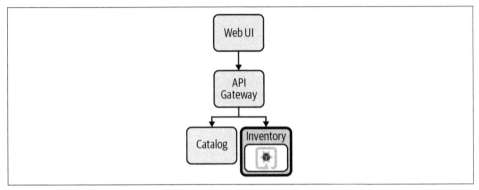

*Figure 2-3. Inventory Quarkus microservice*

You can find all the source code for this example in the book's GitHub repository (*https://oreil.ly/zqbWB*).

## Create Quarkus Maven Project

With Quarkus, you can scaffold a new project either with Maven or Gradle.

 Both Maven and Gradle are popular ways to set up a Java project and manage all dependencies. They differ in their dependency management strategy and they have different configuration formats (XML versus Kotlin DSL), but they are mostly equivalent in terms of capabilities. In this book, we will use Maven as it has wider support through IDEs and tools.

We set up a new Maven project using quarkus-maven-plugin with this command:

```
mvn io.quarkus:quarkus-maven-plugin:2.1.4.Final:create \
    -DprojectGroupId=com.redhat.cloudnative \
    -DprojectArtifactId=inventory-quarkus \
    -DprojectVersion=1.0.0-SNAPSHOT \
    -DclassName="com.redhat.cloudnative.InventoryResource" \
    -Dextensions="quarkus-resteasy,quarkus-resteasy-jsonb,↵
    quarkus-hibernate-orm-panache,quarkus-jdbc-h2"
```

You can also bootstrap a Quarkus app with the online configurator available at *https://code.quarkus.io.*

This will create a skeleton project with an `InventoryResource` class that we will use for implementing our ecommerce Inventory microservice.

Let's have a look at the generated *pom.xml* file:

```xml
<?xml version="1.0" encoding="UTF-8"?>
<project>
    <modelVersion>4.0.0</modelVersion>
    <groupId>com.redhat.cloudnative</groupId> ❶
    <artifactId>inventory-quarkus</artifactId>
    <version>1.0.0-SNAPSHOT</version>
    <properties>
        <quarkus-plugin.version>2.1.4.Final</quarkus-plugin.version>
        <quarkus.platform.artifact-id>quarkus-bom</quarkus.platform.artifact-id>
        <quarkus.platform.group-id>io.quarkus</quarkus.platform.group-id>
        <quarkus.platform.version>2.1.4.Final</quarkus.platform.version>
        <compiler-plugin.version>3.8.1</compiler-plugin.version>
        <surefire-plugin.version>3.0.0-M5</surefire-plugin.version>
        <project.build.sourceEncoding>UTF-8</project.build.sourceEncoding>
        <maven.compiler.source>11</maven.compiler.source>
        <maven.compiler.target>11</maven.compiler.target>
        <maven.compiler.parameters>true</maven.compiler.parameters>
    </properties>
    <dependencyManagement>
        <dependencies>
            <dependency>
                <groupId>io.quarkus</groupId>
                <artifactId>quarkus-bom</artifactId> ❷
                <version>${quarkus.platform.version}</version>
                <type>pom</type>
                <scope>import</scope>
            </dependency>
        </dependencies>
    </dependencyManagement>
    <dependencies> ❸
        <dependency>
          <groupId>io.quarkus</groupId>
          <artifactId>quarkus-resteasy</artifactId>
        </dependency>
        <dependency>
          <groupId>io.quarkus</groupId>
          <artifactId>quarkus-junit5</artifactId>
          <scope>test</scope>
        </dependency>
        <dependency>
          <groupId>io.rest-assured</groupId>
```

```xml
                <artifactId>rest-assured</artifactId>
                <scope>test</scope>
            </dependency>
            <dependency>
                <groupId>io.quarkus</groupId>
                <artifactId>quarkus-resteasy-jsonb</artifactId>
            </dependency>
            <dependency>
                <groupId>io.quarkus</groupId>
                <artifactId>quarkus-hibernate-orm-panache</artifactId>
            </dependency>
            <dependency>
                <groupId>io.quarkus</groupId>
                <artifactId>quarkus-jdbc-h2</artifactId>
            </dependency>
        </dependencies>
...
                <build>
                    <plugins>
                        <plugin>
                            <groupId>io.quarkus</groupId>
                            <artifactId>quarkus-maven-plugin</artifactId>    ❹
                            <version>${quarkus-plugin.version}</version>
                            <executions>
                                <execution>
                                    <goals>
                                        <goal>native-image</goal>
                                    </goals>
                                    <configuration>
                                        <enableHttpUrlHandler>true↵
                                        </enableHttpUrlHandler>
                                    </configuration>
                                </execution>
                            </executions>
                        </plugin>
...
        </profiles>
</project>
```

❶ Here we set up groupId, artifactId, and version. For a full list of available options, please see Table 2-1.

❷ Here you find the import of the Quarkus BOM, allowing you to omit the version on the different Quarkus dependencies.

❸ Here you find all the dependencies for the project, which we expressed as extensions to add. We've included:

- JSON REST Services: This allows you to develop REST services (*https://oreil.ly/hsHvV*) to consume and produce JSON payloads.

- Hibernate ORM Panache: The de facto JPA implementation offers you the full breadth of an Object Relational Mapper. Hibernate ORM with Panache (*https://oreil.ly/zqJDh*) focuses on simplifying the Hibernate-based Persistence layer, making your entities easier to write and maintain.
- Datasources (H2): Datasources (*https://oreil.ly/Q5nGV*) are the main way of obtaining connections to a database; in this example, we will use H2, an in-memory database ready to use for Java apps.

❹ The `quarkus-maven-plugin`, which is responsible for the packaging of the application and also for providing the development mode.

*Table 2-1. Quarkus Maven Project Options*

| Attribute | Default Value | Description |
|---|---|---|
| projectGroupId | com.red hat.cloudnative | The group id of the created project. |
| projectArtifactId | *mandatory* | The artifact id of the created project. Not passing it triggers the interactive mode. |
| projectVersion | 1.0-SNAPSHOT | The version of the created project. |
| platformGroupId | io.quarkus | The group id of the target platform. Given that all the existing platforms are coming from io.quarkus, this one won't be used explicitly. But it's still an option. |
| platformArtifactId | quarkus-universe-bom | The artifact id of the target platform BOM. It should be quarkus-bom in order to use the locally built Quarkus. |
| platformVersion | If it's not specified, the latest one will be resolved. | The version of the platform you want the project to use. It can also accept a version range, in which case the latest from the specified range will be used. |
| className | *Not created if omitted* | The fully qualified name of the generated resource. |
| path | /hello | The resource path, only relevant if className is set. |
| extensions | [] | The list of extensions to add to the project (comma-separated). |

To check all the extensions available, use this command from project dir: `./mvnw quarkus:list-extensions`.

# Create a Domain Model

It's time to write some code now and create a *domain model* and a RESTful endpoint to create the Inventory service. Domain model is a popular pattern in software engineering, and it also fits very well in the cloud native world. The level of abstraction given by the pattern makes it still valid as an object-oriented way of modeling microservices business logic.

You can find the domain model definition in the `Inventory` class in this book's Git-Hub repository (*https://oreil.ly/JE6CD*).

Our domain model implementation consists of an `Entity` mapped to the Persistence layer, representing an inventory of items:

```
package com.redhat.cloudnative;

import javax.persistence.Entity;
import javax.persistence.Table;

import io.quarkus.hibernate.orm.panache.PanacheEntity;

import javax.persistence.Column;

@Entity ❶
@Table(name = "INVENTORY") ❷
public class Inventory extends PanacheEntity{ ❸

    @Column
    public int quantity; ❸

    @Override
    public String toString() {
        return "Inventory [Id='" + id + '\'' + ", quantity=" + quantity + ']';
    }
}
```

❶  `@Entity` marks the class as a JPA entity.

❷  `@Table` customizes the table creation process by defining a table name and database constraint in this case it is `INVENTORY`.

❸  Quarkus will generate `getter/setter` for you when using public attributes and when you extend `PanacheEntity`. Additionally, you have an `id` attribute automatically added.

Once we define the model, we can update our Properties expressed in the *application.properties* file in order to provide the instructions on how to populate data for our microservice:

```
quarkus.datasource.jdbc.url=jdbc:h2:mem:inventory;↳
DB_CLOSE_ON_EXIT=FALSE;DB_CLOSE_DELAY=-1 ❶
quarkus.datasource.db-kind=h2
quarkus.hibernate-orm.database.generation=drop-and-create
quarkus.hibernate-orm.log.sql=true
quarkus.hibernate-orm.sql-load-script=import.sql ❷
%prod.quarkus.package.uber-jar=true ❸
```

❶ JDBC path for the in-memory DB; this can be changed for other types of DB like any RDBMS.

❷ A SQL script that we'll use to populate the Coolstore with some data:
```
INSERT INTO INVENTORY(id, quantity) VALUES (100000, 0);
INSERT INTO INVENTORY(id, quantity) VALUES (329299, 35);
INSERT INTO INVENTORY(id, quantity) VALUES (329199, 12);
INSERT INTO INVENTORY(id, quantity) VALUES (165613, 45);
INSERT INTO INVENTORY(id, quantity) VALUES (165614, 87);
INSERT INTO INVENTORY(id, quantity) VALUES (165954, 43);
INSERT INTO INVENTORY(id, quantity) VALUES (444434, 32);
INSERT INTO INVENTORY(id, quantity) VALUES (444435, 53);
```

❸ An uber-jar contains all the dependencies required packaged in the jar to enable running the application with java -jar. By default, in Quarkus, the generation of the uber-jar is disabled. With the %prod prefix, this option is only activated when building the jar intended for deployments.

## Create a RESTful Service

Quarkus uses the JAX-RS standard for building REST services. When scaffolding a new project as we saw before, a *hello* example service is created in the *className* path we defined. Now we want to expose REST service to retrieve the number of available items in the store from the inventory, using the following:

- Path: */api/inventory/{itemId}*;
- HTTP Method: GET

This returns the quantity for a given item id present in the inventory database.

Let's change the InventoryResource class definition as follows:

```
package com.redhat.cloudnative;

import javax.enterprise.context.ApplicationScoped;
import javax.ws.rs.GET;
import javax.ws.rs.Path;
import javax.ws.rs.PathParam;
import javax.ws.rs.Produces;
import javax.ws.rs.core.MediaType;

@Path("/api/inventory")
@ApplicationScoped
public class InventoryResource {
```

```
@GET
@Path("/{itemId}")
@Produces(MediaType.APPLICATION_JSON)
public Inventory getAvailability(@PathParam("itemId") long itemId) {
    Inventory inventory = Inventory.findById(itemId); ❶
    return inventory;
}
}
```

❶ By extending `PanacheEntity`, we're using the active record persistence pattern instead of a Data Access Obect (DAO). This means that all persistence methods are blended with our own `Entity`.

We just implemented a parametric REST endpoint for our microservice, serving the JSON representation of the items contained in our Coolstore. In this way we provided a layer to query via HTTP `GET` requests our `Inventory Data Model` we implemented in the previous step.

 With Quarkus, there is no need to create an `Application` class. It's supported, but not required. In addition, only one instance of the resource is created and not one per request. You can configure this using the different Scoped annotations (`ApplicationScoped`, `RequestScoped`, etc).

## Run the App in Dev Mode

Development mode in Quarkus is one of the coolest features we have today for cloud native Java development. It enables hot deployment with background compilation, which means that when you modify your Java files or your resource files and then refresh your browser, the changes automatically take effect. This also works for resource files such as the configuration property file. In addition, refreshing the browser triggers a scan of the workspace, and if any changes are detected, the Java files are recompiled and the application is redeployed; your request is then serviced by the redeployed application. If there are any issues with compilation or deployment, an error page will let you know.

You can start the app in dev mode with a built-in Maven goal named `quarkus:dev`. It enables hot deployment with background compilation, which means that when you modify your Java files or your resource files and refresh your browser, these changes will automatically take effect. This also works for resource files like the configuration property file:

```
./mvnw compile quarkus:dev
```

After you start the app in dev mode, you should see an output like this:

```
...
Hibernate:

    drop table if exists INVENTORY CASCADE
Hibernate:

    create table INVENTORY (
       id bigint not null,
        quantity integer,
        primary key (id)
    )

Hibernate:
    INSERT INTO INVENTORY(id, quantity) VALUES (100000, 0)
Hibernate:
    INSERT INTO INVENTORY(id, quantity) VALUES (329299, 35)
Hibernate:
    INSERT INTO INVENTORY(id, quantity) VALUES (329199, 12)
Hibernate:
    INSERT INTO INVENTORY(id, quantity) VALUES (165613, 45)
Hibernate:
    INSERT INTO INVENTORY(id, quantity) VALUES (165614, 87)
Hibernate:
    INSERT INTO INVENTORY(id, quantity) VALUES (165954, 43)
Hibernate:
    INSERT INTO INVENTORY(id, quantity) VALUES (444434, 32)
Hibernate:
    INSERT INTO INVENTORY(id, quantity) VALUES (444435, 53)

__  _____  __  ____   __  __ ____  ____
--/ __ \/ / / / _ | / _ \/ //_/ / / / _/
-/ /_/ / /_/ / __ |/ , _/ ,< / /_/ /\ \
--_____/_/ |_/_/|_/_/|_|\____/___/
2020-12-02 13:11:16,565 INFO  [io.quarkus] (Quarkus Main Thread)↳
inventory-quarkus 1.0.0-SNAPSHOT on JVM (powered by Quarkus 1.7.2.Final)↳
started in 1.487s. Listening on: http://0.0.0.0:8080
2020-12-02 13:11:16,575 INFO  [io.quarkus] (Quarkus Main Thread)↳
Profile dev activated. Live Coding activated.
2020-12-02 13:11:16,575 INFO  [io.quarkus] (Quarkus Main Thread)↳
Installed features: [agroal, cdi, hibernate-orm, jdbc-h2, mutiny, narayana-jta,↳
resteasy, resteasy-jsonb, smallrye-context-propagation]
```

From the output, you can see that Hibernate created a database with the name of our domain model and populated it with some initial data defined in our Properties file.

When we scaffolded the project at the beginning of this chapter, we included a series of dependencies like Panache and used it to map our data model as Entity into a database.

We can also see that our app is up and running, listening to port 8080. If you open your browser now at *http://localhost:8080*, you will see a Quarkus welcome page (as in Figure 2-4).

*Figure 2-4. Quarkus welcome page*

 You can stop the app running in Dev mode by using Ctrl-C from the same terminal where you launched it. When you run Quarkus 2 in Dev mode, it enables by default the Continuous Testing feature, where tests run immediately after code changes have been saved.

You can now try querying one of the items we inserted from the *import.sql* file to test if our microservice is running properly.

Just navigate to *http://localhost:8080/api/inventory/329299*.

You should have the following output:

```
{
    "id":"329299",
    "quantity":35
}
```

The REST API returned a JSON object representing the inventory count for this product. Congratulations on your first cloud native microservice with Quarkus!

We are now going to develop the other microservices that will consume this one, so leave this open in order to have the Coolstore up and running at the end of this chapter.

# Create a Catalog Microservice with Spring Boot

Spring Boot (*https://spring.io/projects/spring-boot*) is an opinionated framework that makes it easy to create stand-alone Spring-based (*https://spring.io*) applications with embedded web containers such as Tomcat (or JBoss Web Server), Jetty, and Undertow that you can run directly on the JVM using `java -jar`. Spring Boot also allows production of a war file that can be deployed on stand-alone web containers.

The opinionated approach means many choices about Spring platform and third-party libraries are already made by Spring Boot so that you can get started with minimum effort and configuration.

Spring Boot is very popular for cloud native Java development because, quoting the official website, it makes it easy to create stand-alone, production-grade Spring-based applications (*https://oreil.ly/KYWe5*) that you can "just run." We will include Spring Boot in our architecture for a Catalog microservice (as shown in Figure 2-5).

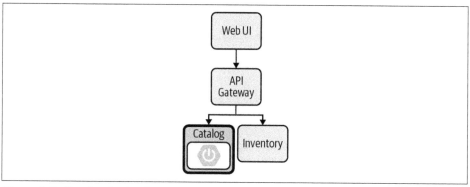

*Figure 2-5. Catalog Spring Boot microservice*

You can find all the source code for creating the Spring Boot microservice in the book's GitHub repository (*https://oreil.ly/M8ya6*).

## Create a Maven Project

Also in this case you can bootstrap your Spring Boot project either with Maven or Gradle. The easiest way to do this is with Spring Initializr (*https://start.spring.io*), an online configurator that helps generate the project structure with all the dependencies needed.

In this case, we will use a Red Hat-supported Spring Boot version from Red Hat Maven repositories (*https://oreil.ly/mAJRs*), using the Project Metadata defined in Table 2-2.

*Table 2-2. Spring Boot Maven Project Options*

| Key | Value | Description |
| --- | --- | --- |
| modelVersion | 4.0.0 | POM model version (always 4.0.0). |
| groupId | com.redhat.cloudnative | Group or organization that the project belongs to. Often expressed as an inverted domain name. |
| artifactId | catalog | Name to be given to the project's library artifact (for example, the name of its JAR or WAR file). |
| version | 1.0-SNAPSHOT | Version of the project that is being built. |
| name | CoolStore Catalog Service | Name of the app. |
| description | CoolStore Catalog Service with Spring Boot | A description for the app. |

Let's have a look at our *pom.xml* file:

```xml
<?xml version="1.0" encoding="UTF-8"?>
<project
  xmlns="http://maven.apache.org/POM/4.0.0"
  xmlns:xsi="http://www.w3.org/2001/XMLSchema-instance"↲
  xsi:schemaLocation="http://maven.apache.org/POM/4.0.0↲
  http://maven.apache.org/xsd/maven-4.0.0.xsd">
  <modelVersion>4.0.0</modelVersion>
  <groupId>com.redhat.cloudnative</groupId> ❶
  <artifactId>catalog</artifactId>
  <version>1.0-SNAPSHOT</version>
  <name>CoolStore Catalog Service</name>
  <description>CoolStore Catalog Service with Spring Boot</description>
  <properties>
    <spring-boot.version>2.1.6.SP3-redhat-00001</spring-boot.version> ❷
    <spring-boot.maven.plugin.version>2.1.4.RELEASE-redhat-00001↲
    </spring-boot.maven.plugin.version>
    <spring.k8s.bom.version>1.0.3.RELEASE</spring.k8s.bom.version>
    <fabric8.maven.plugin.version>4.3.0</fabric8.maven.plugin.version>
  </properties>
  <repositories>
    <repository>
      <id>redhat-ga</id>
      <url>https://maven.repository.redhat.com/ga/</url>
    </repository>
  </repositories>
  <pluginRepositories>
    <pluginRepository>
      <id>redhat-ga-plugins</id>
      <url>https://maven.repository.redhat.com/ga/</url>
    </pluginRepository>
```

```xml
    </pluginRepositories>
    <dependencyManagement>
      <dependencies>
        <dependency>
          <groupId>me.snowdrop</groupId>
          <artifactId>spring-boot-bom</artifactId>
          <version>${spring-boot.version}</version>
          <type>pom</type>
          <scope>import</scope>
        </dependency>
        <dependency>
          <groupId>org.springframework.cloud</groupId>
          <artifactId>spring-cloud-kubernetes-dependencies</artifactId>
          <version>${spring.k8s.bom.version}</version>
          <type>pom</type>
          <scope>import</scope>
        </dependency>
      </dependencies>
    </dependencyManagement>
    <dependencies> ❸
      <dependency>
        <groupId>org.springframework.boot</groupId>
        <artifactId>spring-boot-starter-web</artifactId>
      </dependency>
      <dependency>
        <groupId>org.springframework.boot</groupId>
        <artifactId>spring-boot-starter-data-jpa</artifactId>
      </dependency>
      <dependency>
        <groupId>org.springframework.boot</groupId>
        <artifactId>spring-boot-starter-actuator</artifactId>
      </dependency>
      <dependency>
        <groupId>org.springframework.cloud</groupId>
        <artifactId>spring-cloud-starter-kubernetes-config</artifactId>
      </dependency>
      <dependency>
        <groupId>com.h2database</groupId>
        <artifactId>h2</artifactId>
      </dependency>
    </dependencies>
...
</project>
```

❶ Project metadata we generated by Initializr or manually

❷ Spring Boot version used

❸ Dependencies we need:

- JPA: Spring Data with JPA

- Spring Cloud (*https://oreil.ly/n4oSG*): support and tooling from Spring for cloud native Java apps
- H2: an in-memory database that we will use for this purpose

This is a minimal Spring Boot project with support for RESTful services and Spring Data with JPA for connecting to a database. Any new project contains no code other than the main class, in this case, the `CatalogApplication` class, which is there to bootstrap the Spring Boot application.

You can find it in this book's GitHub repository (*https://oreil.ly/FK15g*):

```
package com.redhat.cloudnative.catalog;

import org.springframework.boot.SpringApplication;
import org.springframework.boot.autoconfigure.SpringBootApplication;

@SpringBootApplication ❶
public class CatalogApplication {

    public static void main(String[] args) {
        SpringApplication.run(CatalogApplication.class, args);
    }
}
```

❶ A convenience annotation that adds autoconfiguration and component scan, and also enables defining extra configurations. It is equivalent to using `@Configuration`, `@EnableAutoConfiguration`, and `@ComponentScan` with their default attributes.

## Create a Domain Model

Next, we need to provide some data to consume for our microservice representing the catalog of our Coolstore ecommerce website. Also here, we define a domain model for the high-level interaction with the Persistence layer, and an interface that enables the communication between a REST endpoint to expose the service and the data model (as shown in Figure 2-6).

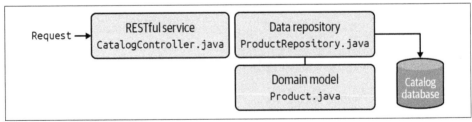

*Figure 2-6. Data model flow*

The database is configured using the Spring application configuration file, which is located in the properties file `application.properties`. Let's have a look at this file to see the database connection details.

You can find it in this book's GitHub repository (*https://oreil.ly/cRnE6*):

```
spring.application.name=catalog
server.port=8080
spring.datasource.url=jdbc:h2:mem:catalog;DB_CLOSE_ON_EXIT=FALSE ❶
spring.datasource.username=sa
spring.datasource.password=
spring.datasource.driver-class-name=org.h2.Driver ❷
```

❶ JDBC URL for H2 DB

❷ Use of H2 in-memory database

Let's create our domain model, which is similar to the one we created for the Inventory microservice before.

You can find it in this book's GitHub repository (*https://oreil.ly/s971w*):

```
package com.redhat.cloudnative.catalog;

import java.io.Serializable;

import javax.persistence.Entity;
import javax.persistence.Id;
import javax.persistence.Table;

@Entity ❶
@Table(name = "PRODUCT") ❷
public class Product implements Serializable {

    private static final long serialVersionUID = 1L;

    @Id ❸
    private String itemId;

    private String name;

    private String description;

    private double price;

    public Product() {
    }

    public String getItemId() {
        return itemId;
    }
```

```
  public void setItemId(String itemId) {
    this.itemId = itemId;
  }

  public String getName() {
    return name;
  }

  public void setName(String name) {
    this.name = name;
  }

  public String getDescription() {
    return description;
  }

  public void setDescription(String description) {
    this.description = description;
  }

  public double getPrice() {
    return price;
  }

  public void setPrice(double price) {
    this.price = price;
  }

  @Override
  public String toString() {
    return "Product [itemId=" + itemId + ", name=" + name
      + ", price=" + price + "]";
  }
}
```

❶   @Entity marks the class as a JPA entity.

❷   @Table customizes the table creation process by defining a table name and data-base constraint, in this case a table named *CATALOG*.

❸   @Id marks the primary key for the table.

## Create a Data Repository

Spring Data repository abstraction simplifies dealing with data models in Spring applications by reducing the amount of boilerplate code required to implement data access layers for various persistence stores. Repository and its subinterfaces (*https:// oreil.ly/wUh7w*) are the central concept in Spring Data, which is a marker interface to provide data manipulation functionality for the entity class that is being managed.

When the application starts, Spring finds all interfaces marked as repositories and for each interface found, the infrastructure configures the required persistent technologies and provides an implementation for the repository interface.

We will now create a new Java interface named ProductRepository in the com.red hat.cloudnative.catalog package and extend the CrudRepository interface (*https://oreil.ly/gPUjj*) in order to indicate to Spring that you want to expose a complete set of methods to manipulate the entity.

You can find it in this book's GitHub repository (*https://oreil.ly/CIGc5*):

```java
package com.redhat.cloudnative.catalog;

import org.springframework.data.repository.CrudRepository;

public interface ProductRepository extends CrudRepository<Product, String> { ❶
}
```

❶ CrudRepository (*https://oreil.ly/eRvCG*): interface used to indicate to Spring that we want to expose a complete set of methods to manipulate the entity

Now that we have a domain model and a repository to retrieve the domain model, let's create a RESTful service that returns the list of products.

## Create a RESTful Service

Spring Boot uses Spring Web MVC as the default RESTful stack in Spring applications. We will now create a new Java class named CatalogController in the com.red hat.cloudnative.catalog package for that, exposing a REST endpoint. We'll use the following:

- Path: */api/catalog/*
- HTTP Method: GET

This returns a catalog for all items available in the store, matching items from Inventory service with data from Catalog service.

You can find it in this book's GitHub repository (*https://oreil.ly/SjQ4h*):

```java
package com.redhat.cloudnative.catalog;

import java.util.List;
import java.util.Spliterator;
import java.util.stream.Collectors;
import java.util.stream.StreamSupport;

import org.springframework.beans.factory.annotation.Autowired;
import org.springframework.http.MediaType;
import org.springframework.web.bind.annotation.GetMapping;
```

```
import org.springframework.web.bind.annotation.RequestMapping;
import org.springframework.web.bind.annotation.ResponseBody;
import org.springframework.web.bind.annotation.RestController;

@RestController
@RequestMapping(value = "/api/catalog") ❶
public class CatalogController {

    @Autowired ❷
    private ProductRepository repository; ❸

    @ResponseBody
    @GetMapping(produces = MediaType.APPLICATION_JSON_VALUE)
    public List<Product> getAll() {
        Spliterator<Product> products = repository.findAll().spliterator();
        return
          StreamSupport.stream(products, false).collect(Collectors.toList());
    }
}
```

❶ @RequestMapping indicates the above REST service defines an endpoint that is accessible via HTTP GET at */api/catalog*.

❷ Spring Boot automatically provides an implementation for `ProductRepository` at runtime and injects it into the controller using the `@Autowired` annotation (*https://oreil.ly/nuvh0*).

❸ The `repository` attribute on the controller class is used to retrieve the list of products from the databases.

Everything is now ready to start our second microservice, which will listen to port 9000 to avoid conflicts with the other one:

```
mvn spring-boot:run
```

You should see an output like this:

```
[INFO] --- spring-boot-maven-plugin:2.1.4.RELEASE-redhat-00001:run (default-cli)
↳ @ catalog ---
[INFO] Attaching agents: []
2020-12-02 17:12:18.528  INFO 61053 --- [           main]↳
trationDelegate$BeanPostProcessorChecker : Bean 'org.springframework.cloud.auto
configure.ConfigurationPropertiesRebinderAutoConfiguration' of type [org.
springframework.cloud.autoconfigure.ConfigurationPropertiesRebinder
AutoConfiguration$$EnhancerBySpringCGLIB$$e898759c] is not eligible for getting
processed by all BeanPostProcessors (for example: not eligible for auto-proxying)
```

```
  .   ___
 /\\ / ___'_ __ _ _(_)_ __  __ _ \ \ \ \
( ( )\___ | '_ | '_| | '_ \/ _` | \ \ \ \
 \\/  ___)| |_)| | | | | || (_| |  ) ) ) )
  '  |____| .__|_| |_|_| |_\__, | / / / /
 =========|_|==============|___/=/_/_/_/
 :: Spring Boot ::        (v2.1.6.RELEASE)
StandardService   : Starting service [Tomcat]
2020-12-02 17:12:20.064  INFO 61053 --- [        main]↳
org.apache.catalina.core.StandardEngine  : Starting Servlet Engine:
  Apache Tomcat/9.0.7.redhat-16
2020-12-02 17:12:20.220  INFO 61053 --- [        main]↳
o.a.c.c.C.[Tomcat].[localhost].[/]        : Initializing Spring embedded
  WebApplicationContext
2020-12-02 17:12:20.220  INFO 61053 --- [        main]↳
...
```

Your app is now listening on port *9000* to the endpoint we configured; you can verify it by navigating to *http://localhost:9000/api/catalog*.

You should see this output from the REST API returning a JSON object representing the product list:

```
[
    {
        "itemId":"100000",
        "name":"Red Fedora",
        "description":"Official Red Hat Fedora",
        "price":34.99
    },
    {
        "itemId":"329299",
        "name":"Quarkus T-shirt",
        "description":"This updated unisex essential fits like a well-loved
        favorite,↳ featuring a crew neck, short sleeves and designed with superior
        combed and↳ ring- spun cotton.",
        "price":10.0
    },
    {
        "itemId":"329199",
        "name":"Pronounced Kubernetes",
        "description":"Kubernetes is changing how enterprises work in the cloud.↳
        But one of the biggest questions people have is: How do you pronounce it?",
        "price":9.0
    },
    {
        "itemId":"165613",
        "name":"Knit socks",
        "description":"Your brand will get noticed on these full color knit
        socks.↳ Imported.",
        "price":4.15
    },
    {
```

```
        "itemId":"165614",
        "name":"Quarkus H2Go water bottle",
        "description":"Sporty 16. 9 oz double wall stainless steel thermal bottle↳
        with copper vacuum insulation, and threaded insulated lid. Imprinted.
        Imported.",
        "price":14.45
    },
    {
        "itemId":"165954",
        "name":"Patagonia Refugio pack 28L",
        "description":"Made from 630-denier 100% nylon (50% recycled / 50%
        high-tenacity)↳ plain weave; lined with 200-denier 100% recycled polyester.
        ...",
        "price":6.0
    },
    {
        "itemId":"444434",
        "name":"Red Hat Impact T-shirt",
        "description":"This 4. 3 ounce, 60% combed ringspun cotton/40% polyester↳
        jersey t- shirt features a slightly heathered appearance. The fabric↳
        laundered for reduced shrinkage. Next Level brand apparel. Printed.",
        "price":9.0
    },
    {
        "itemId":"444435",
        "name":"Quarkus twill cap",
        "description":"100% cotton chino twill cap with an unstructured,
        low-profile,↳ six-panel design. The crown measures 3 1/8 and this
        features a Permacurv↳ visor and a buckle closure with a grommet.",
        "price":13.0
    },
    {
        "itemId":"444437",
        "name":"Nanobloc Universal Webcam Cover",
        "description":"NanoBloc Webcam Cover fits phone, laptop, desktop, PC,↳
        MacBook Pro, iMac, ...",
        "price":2.75
    }
]
```

 The output has been formatted in *pretty* mode in the book's code listing. You'll notice the combination of our items from the Quarkus Inventory microservice with the description and the price from the Spring Boot Catalog microservice. If you recall the info from the previous test with item 329299, it's a Quarkus T-shirt.

Congratulations on creating your second microservice; now it's time to connect a frontend to our backends. In order to do it, we will use a software API gateway with reactive Java in the next section.

# Create a Gateway Service with Vert.x

Eclipse Vert.x (*https://vertx.io*) is an event-driven toolkit for building reactive applications on the Java Virtual Machine (JVM). Vert.x does not impose a specific framework or packaging model; it can be used within your existing applications and frameworks in order to add reactive functionality by just adding the Vert.x jar files to the application classpath.

Eclipse Vert.x enables building reactive systems as defined by The Reactive Manifesto (*https://oreil.ly/jCg8t*) and builds services that are:

- Responsive: to handle requests in a reasonable time

- Resilient: to stay responsive in the face of failures

- Elastic: to stay responsive under various loads and be able to scale up and down

- Message-driven: components interact using asynchronous message passing

It is designed to be event-driven and nonblocking. In fact, events are delivered into an event loop that must never be blocked. Unlike traditional applications, Vert.x uses a very small number of threads responsible for dispatching the events to event handlers. If the event loop is blocked, the events won't be delivered anymore and therefore the code needs to be mindful of this execution model (as shown in Figure 2-7).

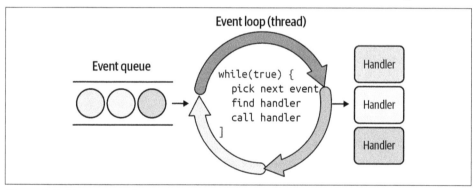

*Figure 2-7. Vert.x event loop*

In our architecture, this microservice will act as an asynchronous software API gateway, developed as a reactive Java microservice that efficiently routes and dispatches the traffic to the Inventory and Catalog component of our cloud native ecommerce website, as displayed in Figure 2-8.

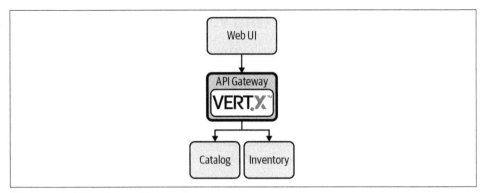

*Figure 2-8. API gateway Vert.x microservice*

You can find the source code of this microservice in this book's GitHub repository (*https://oreil.ly/6pe8n*).

## Create a Vert.x Maven Project

Vert.x supports both Maven and Gradle, and the easiest way to bootstrap a new Vert.x Maven project is through a template project structure offered by the Vert.x community (*https://oreil.ly/fuaVI*). In our case, we are using Red Hat Maven repositories and added the settings shown in Table 2-3.

*Table 2-3. Vert.x Maven Project Options*

| Key | Value | Description |
| --- | --- | --- |
| modelVersion | 4.0.0 | POM model version (always 4.0.0). |
| groupId | com.redhat.cloud native | Group or organization that the project belongs to. Often expressed as an inverted domain name. |
| artifactId | gateway | Name to be given to the project's library artifact (a JAR in this case). |
| version | 1.0-SNAPSHOT | Version of the project that is being built. |
| name | CoolStore Gate way Service | Name of the app. |

Let's have a look at how the *pom.xml* will look:

```
<?xml version="1.0" encoding="UTF-8"?>
<project xmlns="http://maven.apache.org/POM/4.0.0"↩
xmlns:xsi="http://www.w3.org/2001/XMLSchema-instance"↩
xsi:schemaLocation="http://maven.apache.org/POM/4.0.0
  http://maven.apache.org/xsd/maven-4.0.0.xsd">
    <modelVersion>4.0.0</modelVersion> ❶
    <groupId>com.redhat.cloudnative</groupId>
    <artifactId>gateway</artifactId>
    <version>1.0-SNAPSHOT</version>
    <packaging>jar</packaging>
```

```
<name>CoolStore Gateway Service</name>
<description>CoolStore Gateway Service with Eclipse Vert.x</description>

<properties>
    <vertx.version>3.6.3.redhat-00009</vertx.version> ❷
    <vertx-maven-plugin.version>1.0.15</vertx-maven-plugin.version>
    <vertx.verticle>com.redhat.cloudnative.gateway.GatewayVerticle↵
    </vertx.verticle> ❸
    <fabric8.maven.plugin.version>4.3.0</fabric8.maven.plugin.version>
    <slf4j.version>1.7.21</slf4j.version>
</properties>
...
<dependencyManagement>
    <dependencies>
        <dependency>
            <groupId>io.vertx</groupId>
            <artifactId>vertx-dependencies</artifactId>
            <version>${vertx.version}</version>
            <type>pom</type>
            <scope>import</scope>
        </dependency>
    </dependencies>
</dependencyManagement>

<dependencies> ❹
    <dependency>
        <groupId>io.vertx</groupId>
        <artifactId>vertx-core</artifactId>
    </dependency>
    <dependency>
        <groupId>io.vertx</groupId>
        <artifactId>vertx-config</artifactId>
    </dependency>
    <dependency>
        <groupId>io.vertx</groupId>
        <artifactId>vertx-web</artifactId>
    </dependency>
    <dependency>
        <groupId>io.vertx</groupId>
        <artifactId>vertx-web-client</artifactId>
    </dependency>
    <dependency>
        <groupId>io.vertx</groupId>
        <artifactId>vertx-rx-java2</artifactId>
    </dependency>
    <dependency>
        <groupId>io.vertx</groupId>
        <artifactId>vertx-health-check</artifactId>
    </dependency>
    <dependency>
        <groupId>org.slf4j</groupId>
        <artifactId>slf4j-api</artifactId>
```

```
            <version>${slf4j.version}</version>
        </dependency>
        <dependency>
            <groupId>org.slf4j</groupId>
            <artifactId>slf4j-jdk14</artifactId>
            <version>${slf4j.version}</version>
        </dependency>
    </dependencies>
    ...
</project>
```

❶ Project metadata

❷ Vert.x version used

❸ `GatewayVerticle`: the name of the main verticle; it's the entry point for our app

❹ A list of dependecies:

- Vert.x libraries: *vertx-core, vertx-config, vertx-web, vertx-web-client*
- Rx support for Vert.x (*https://oreil.ly/ynXXu*): vertx-rx-java2

## Create an API Gateway

Next, we want to create an API gateway as the entry point for the web frontend of our website, to access all backend services from a single place. This pattern is predictably called API gateway (*https://oreil.ly/6oZaE*) and is a common practice in microservices architecture.

The unit of deployment in Vert.x is called a *verticle*. A verticle processes incoming events over an event loop, where events can be anything such as receiving network buffers, timing events, or messages sent by other verticles.

We define our main verticle as GatewayVerticle as we declared it previously in the *pom.xml*, and expose the REST endpoint that will be routed to the Catalog /api/catalog:

- Path: */api/catalog/*
- HTTP Method: `GET`

This routes the traffic to Catalog and returns a JSON object containing all items available in the store, matching items from Inventory service with data from Catalog service.

You can find it in this book's GitHub repository (*https://oreil.ly/vkevU*):

```
package com.redhat.cloudnative.gateway;
```

```
import io.vertx.core.http.HttpMethod;
import io.vertx.core.json.JsonArray;
import io.vertx.core.json.JsonObject;
import io.vertx.ext.web.client.WebClientOptions;
import io.vertx.reactivex.config.ConfigRetriever;
import io.vertx.reactivex.core.AbstractVerticle;
import io.vertx.reactivex.ext.web.Router;
import io.vertx.reactivex.ext.web.RoutingContext;
import io.vertx.reactivex.ext.web.client.WebClient;
import io.vertx.reactivex.ext.web.client.predicate.ResponsePredicate;
import io.vertx.reactivex.ext.web.codec.BodyCodec;
import io.vertx.reactivex.ext.web.handler.CorsHandler;
import io.vertx.reactivex.ext.web.handler.StaticHandler;
import org.slf4j.Logger;
import org.slf4j.LoggerFactory;
import io.reactivex.Observable;
import io.reactivex.Single;

import java.util.ArrayList;
import java.util.List;

public class GatewayVerticle extends AbstractVerticle { ❶
    private static final Logger LOG = LoggerFactory.getLogger(
        GatewayVerticle.class);

    private WebClient catalog;
    private WebClient inventory;

    @Override
    public void start() { ❷
        Router router = Router.router(vertx); ❸
        router.route().handler(CorsHandler.create("*")↵
        .allowedMethod(HttpMethod.GET));
        router.get("/*").handler(StaticHandler.create("assets"));
        router.get("/health").handler(this::health);
        router.get("/api/products").handler(this::products); ❹

        ConfigRetriever retriever = ConfigRetriever.create(vertx);
        retriever.getConfig(ar -> {
            if (ar.failed()) {
                // Failed to retrieve the configuration
            } else {
                JsonObject config = ar.result();

                String catalogApiHost =↵
                config.getString("COMPONENT_CATALOG_HOST", "localhost");
                Integer catalogApiPort =↵
                config.getInteger("COMPONENT_CATALOG_PORT", 9000);

                catalog = WebClient.create(vertx,
                    new WebClientOptions()
                        .setDefaultHost(catalogApiHost)
```

```
            .setDefaultPort(catalogApiPort)); ❺

        LOG.info("Catalog Service Endpoint: " + catalogApiHost↳
        + ":" + catalogApiPort.toString());

        String inventoryApiHost =↳
        config.getString("COMPONENT_INVENTORY_HOST", "localhost");
        Integer inventoryApiPort =↳
        config.getInteger("COMPONENT_INVENTORY_PORT", 8080;

        inventory = WebClient.create(vertx,
            new WebClientOptions()
                .setDefaultHost(inventoryApiHost)
                .setDefaultPort(inventoryApiPort)); ❻

        LOG.info("Inventory Service Endpoint: "↳
        + inventoryApiHost + ":" + inventoryApiPort.toString());

        vertx.createHttpServer()
            .requestHandler(router)
            .listen(Integer.getInteger("http.port", 8090)); ❼

        LOG.info("Server is running on port "↳
        + Integer.getInteger("http.port", 8090));
            }
        });
    }

    private void products(RoutingContext rc) {
...
    }

    private Single<JsonObject> getAvailabilityFromInventory(JsonObject product) {
...
    }

    private void health(RoutingContext rc) {
...
    }
}
```

❶  A Verticle is created by extending from AbstractVerticle class.

❷  The start() method creates an HTTP server.

❸  A Router is retrieved for mapping the REST endpoints.

❹  A REST endpoint is created for mapping /api/catalog Catalog endpoint through a product() function that will retrieve the content.

**❺**  An HTTP Server is created that listens on port 8090.

**❻**  Give `Inventory` microservice a hostname and port to connect to.

**❼**  The microservice supports ENV vars to change its hostname and port from Properties; this is important for the portability of our architecture across clouds.

 We use port 8090 to avoid conflict while running it in local development. The port number can also be changed with a property file as described in the Vert.x Config doc (*https://oreil.ly/OgGIP*). When developing with microservices, the use of environment variables to map hosts and ports is highly encouraged; we use them to map Inventory and Catalog endpoints dynamically.

We are now ready to start our API gateway:

```
mvn compile vertx:run
```

The output should be similar to this:

```
[INFO] Scanning for projects...
[INFO]
[INFO] -----------------< com.redhat.cloudnative:gateway >-----------------
[INFO] Building CoolStore Gateway Service 1.0-SNAPSHOT
[INFO] -----------------------------[ jar ]-----------------------------
[INFO]
[INFO] --- vertx-maven-plugin:1.0.15:initialize (vmp) @ gateway ---
[INFO]
[INFO] --- maven-resources-plugin:2.6:resources (default-resources) @ gateway ---
[WARNING] Using platform encoding (UTF-8 actually) to copy filtered resources,↳
i.e. build is platform dependent!
[INFO] Copying 3 resources
[INFO]
[INFO] --- maven-compiler-plugin:3.6.1:compile (default-compile) @ gateway ---
[INFO] Changes detected - recompiling the module!
[WARNING] File encoding has not been set, using platform encoding UTF-8,↳
i.e. build is platform dependent!
[INFO] Compiling 1 source file to↳
/home/bluesman/git/cloud-native-java2/↳
labs/gateway-vertx/target/classes
...
  com.redhat.cloudnative.gateway.GatewayVerticle↳
lambda$start$0
[INFO] INFO: Catalog Service Endpoint: localhost:9000
[INFO] dic 02, 2020 6:56:56 PM com.redhat.cloudnative.gateway.GatewayVerticle↳
lambda$start$0
[INFO] INFO: Inventory Service Endpoint: localhost:8080
[INFO] dic 02, 2020 6:56:56 PM com.redhat.cloudnative.gateway.GatewayVerticle↳
lambda$start$0
```

```
[INFO] INFO: Server is running on port 8090
[INFO] dic 02, 2020 6:56:56 PM
```

Let's verify it is up and running and correctly routing traffic by navigating to *http://localhost:8090/api/products*.

You should get the JSON object from Catalog's endpoint, in the pretty format:

```
[ {
  "itemId" : "165613",
  "name" : "Knit socks",
  "description" : "Your brand will get noticed on these full color knit socks.↳
  Imported.",
  "price" : 4.15,
  "availability" : {
    "quantity" : 45
  }
}, {
  "itemId" : "165614",
  "name" : "Quarkus H2Go water bottle",
  "description" : "Sporty 16. 9 oz double wall stainless steel thermal bottle↳
  with copper vacuum insulation, and threaded insulated lid. Imprinted.
    Imported.",
  "price" : 14.45,
  "availability" : {
    "quantity" : 87
  }
}, {
  "itemId" : "329199",
  "name" : "Pronounced Kubernetes",
  "description" : "Kubernetes is changing how enterprises work in the cloud.↳
  But one of the biggest questions people have is: How do you pronounce it?",
  "price" : 9.0,
  "availability" : {
    "quantity" : 12
  }
}, {
  "itemId" : "100000",
  "name" : "Red Fedora",
  "description" : "Official Red Hat Fedora",
  "price" : 34.99,
  "availability" : {
    "quantity" : 0
  }
}, {
  "itemId" : "329299",
  "name" : "Quarkus T-shirt",
  "description" : "This updated unisex essential fits like a well-loved favorite,
  ↳ featuring a crew neck, short sleeves and designed with superior combed
  and ring-↳ spun cotton.",
  "price" : 10.0,
  "availability" : {
    "quantity" : 35
```

```
      }
    }, {
      "itemId" : "165954",
      "name" : "Patagonia Refugio pack 28L",
      "description" : "Made from 630-denier 100% nylon (50% recycled/50% ↳
      high-tenacity) plain weave; lined with 200-denier 100% recycled polyester...",
      "price" : 6.0,
      "availability" : {
        "quantity" : 43
      }
    }, {
      "itemId" : "444434",
      "name" : "Red Hat Impact T-shirt",
      "description" : "This 4. 3 ounce, 60% combed ringspun cotton/40% polyester↳
      jersey t- shirt features a slightly heathered appearance. The fabric laundered↳
      for reduced shrinkage. Next Level brand apparel. Printed.",
      "price" : 9.0,
      "availability" : {
        "quantity" : 32
      }
    }, {
      "itemId" : "444437",
      "name" : "Nanobloc Universal Webcam Cover",
      "description" : "NanoBloc Webcam Cover fits phone, laptop, desktop, PC,↳
      MacBook Pro, iMac, ...",
      "price" : 2.75
    }, {
      "itemId" : "444435",
      "name" : "Quarkus twill cap",
      "description" : "100% cotton chino twill cap with an unstructured,
      low-profile,↳ six-panel design. The crown measures 3 1/8 and this features a
      Permacurv↳ visor and a buckle closure with a grommet.",
      "price" : 13.0,
      "availability" : {
        "quantity" : 53
      }
    } ]
```

Our backend is now complete. We are ready to provide some data to show from a nice frontend.

# Create a Frontend with Node.js and AngularJS

Node.js (*https://nodejs.org*) is a popular open source framework for asynchronous event-driven JavaScript development. Even if this is a book about modern Java development, in microservices architecture it is common to have a heterogeneous environment with multiple programming languages and frameworks involved. The challenge here is how to let them communicate efficiently. One solution is having a common interface like API gateway exchanging messages via REST calls or queue systems.

AngularJS is a JavaScript-based frontend web framework whose goal is to simplify both the development and the testing of such applications by providing a framework for client-side model–view–controller (MVC) and model–view–viewmodel (MVVM) architectures, as illustrated in Figure 2-9. When used with Node.js, it provides a fast way to easily bootstrap a frontend.

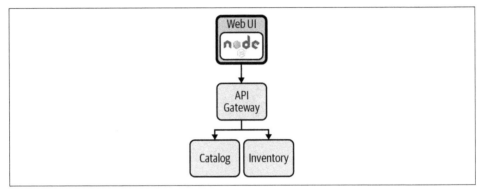

*Figure 2-9. Node.js + AngularJS Dashboard*

You can find the source code of this microservice in this book's GitHub repository (*https://oreil.ly/fv5aa*).

## Run the Frontend

All the HTML and JavaScript code has been prepared, and we are ready to link this frontend to our backends showing our Coolstore app up and running.

### Get NPM

NPM (*https://oreil.ly/aN4J3*) is a package manager for JavaScript, similar to Maven, that will help us download all dependencies and start our frontend.

### Install dependencies

We can resolve all dependencies within the web-nodejs directory and by launching the npm command:

```
npm install
```

You should get an output like this:

```
...
added 1465 packages from 723 contributors and audited 1471 packages in 26.368s

52 packages are looking for funding
  run `npm fund` for details
```

```
found 228 vulnerabilities (222 low, 6 high)
  run `npm audit fix` to fix them, or `npm audit` for details
```

## Start the app

We are now ready to verify if our frontend can correctly consume the backend services through the API gateway, mapping images with the data received. Since we are in local development, we will use the environment variable to change the Node.js default port to avoid conflicts. We will also use an environment variable to map the API gateway REST endpoint, as shown in Table 2-4.

*Table 2-4. Frontend environment variables*

| ENV | Value | Description |
|-----|-------|-------------|
| PORT | 3000 | Global env for Node.js to map the port to use for starting the process; we use 3000 in this case. |
| COOLSTORE_GW_ENDPOINT | http://localhost:8090 | Enviroment variable defined in the frontend to map the API gateway service hostname. |

Start the app with this command:

```
COOLSTORE_GW_ENDPOINT=http://localhost:8090 PORT=3000 npm start
```

Navigate to the address where we exposed our Node.js app at *http://localhost:3000*.

Congratulations! Your cloud native Coolstore ecommerce website is up and running now; you can verify it in Figure 2-10.

*Figure 2-10. Coolstore demo complete*

# Summary

In this chapter, we walked through a complete microservices-based architecture implementation, using different Java frameworks for different components. We gave an overview on how to split the typical monolithic approach into a more diverse and heterogeneous environment, lightweight and ready to run in multiple contexts such as local development or production systems. This is an example of what we call cloud native development.

# CHAPTER 3

# Travel Light on Your Pathway

He who would travel happily must travel light.

—Antoine de Saint-Exupéry

In the last chapter, you built a microservices-based system, and we also showed you some migration steps from an existing application. But the challenge with all examples is that they remove complexity for the sake of easier understandability. What might seem clear for smaller examples becomes challenging with real business systems. In particular, think about complex legacy systems. As outlined in the first chapter, technologies and methodologies developed over the years have led to today's best practices and tools to develop modern enterprise systems. Just because our industry now has a more extensive toolbox with shiny new things to work with doesn't mean you should always use them. If you think about this and our growing number of frameworks, methodologies, and technologies, one question becomes more pressing: What tools and architecture should you use for your next system, and how and where will you run them? Before you can decide, you need to think a bit about the most prominent architectural styles that have emerged for enterprise applications in the last couple of years (Three-tier, Enterprise Integration, service-oriented architecture, microservices, and event-driven architecture).

## Three-Tier or Distributed System

The Enterprise Java world is dominated by monolithic applications. They often are designed as single execution units that scale with server instances and clustering functionality. They are also often referred to as "Three-tier systems" to reflect the three main parts they are composed of: a client-side user interface, a server-side business logic implementation, and server-side data Persistence or Integration layer. The server-side parts are called a "monolith" since they are packaged as a single large executable. Any changes to the system typically involve building and deploying a new version.

 Learn more about building microservices in Sam Newman's excellent book *Building Microservices* (O'Reilly) (*https://oreil.ly/JZqsr*), now in its second edition.

A microservices-based architecture is an approach to developing a single application as a suite of small services, each of them running in its own process and communicating with lightweight mechanisms, often an HTTP resource API or as part of an event-driven architecture (EDA). These services are built around business capabilities and are independently deployable by fully automated deployment machinery. There is a bare minimum of centralized management of these services, which may be written in different programming languages and use different data storage technologies.

The difference between the monolithic and microservice styles can't be more fundamental. And so are the nonfunctional requirements leading to the choice of one. The most critical requirements result from extremely flexible scaling scenarios. As an experienced developer and architect, you know how to evaluate functional and non-functional requirements to conclude your specific project. In this chapter, we will help you navigate your migration approach and target platform. Your journey starts by looking at the motivation for modernization. Let's take a deeper look at what makes us think about modernization in general and where to start looking for opportunities.

## Technology Updates, Modernization, and Transformation

Enterprise software is developed to put business value into code that can be executed within nonfunctional and functional requirements. Creating value depends on our ability to deliver applications quickly. Not only with better quality but also ready to be changed quickly, enabling businesses to respond to new challenges or regulatory changes in the market. And these challenges are multifaceted. First, you address scaling challenges with cloud native applications to handle bigger transaction volumes. New business cases will also require you to analyze data further and might be solved by artificial intelligence (AI) and machine learning (ML). And last but not least, our interconnected world generates more data from the Internet of Things (IoT). What might read like it is a natural progression of architectures isn't. In fact, the evolving business requirements drive modernization and architectural evolution by changing functional and nonfunctional requirements.

Aditionally, you will find operational concerns influencing modernization needs. For example, expiring maintenance contracts or outdated technologies can drive technology updates. The continuously evolving Java language with the shortened release cycles can also influence modernization decisions. Modernization can happen at any level of your project, ranging from the execution environment (e.g., virtual machines to container) to the Java Virtual Machine (JVM version or vendor), individual dependencies, external interfaces, and services.

It is essential to distinguish between three different angles to modernization here. While the *technology updates* within existing processes and boundaries are a familiar and well-established challenge for software projects, modernization refers to something else. Often paired with the word "digital," the term *modernization* refers to adopting new technology. It involves upgrading systems, platforms, and software with new functionality. It can be as simple as taking an existing paper-based process and turning it digital using new software and hardware, or more complex, such as phasing out existing infrastructure and moving to the cloud. Sometimes you'll also hear *transformation* when someone talks about modern systems. Digital transformation means taking advantage of modern technology to reimagine an organization's processes, culture, people, and customer experiences. It can result in new business models, revenue streams, policies, and values. Transformation is somewhat of a holistic lens into an organization with a clear focus to fundamentally change business performance. Modernization is embedded and becomes the centerpiece that software developers and architects need to navigate.

Despite your project-specific reasons to take the first step in modernizing your application, it is essential to remember that modernization itself does not carry any particular mandates for specific target environments or technologies. It is an ever-changing and growing set of candidate technologies that enable companies to compete and grow in their industry. You can find some of them in technology trend reports (e.g., the ThoughtWorks Technology Radar (*https://oreil.ly/SWvEH*)) or on hype cycles (Gartner Hype Cycle (*https://oreil.ly/JT4jE*)). But as you've seen in the first chapter, two of the strongest motivations to constantly innovate are speed and cost pressure. Both are addressed by a modern, cloud native, microservices-based architecture.

## The 6 Rs

Now that you've learned the motivation behind application modernization, you want to identify general approaches to modernization and define a categorization for existing applications. Doing this helps you manage a variety of different applications, especially in a platform modernization project. Rather than looking at the details of a single application, consider the complete runtime architecture of traditional Enterprise Java applications. In that case, you'll commonly identify on-premise hardware, which is usually virtualized and made available to projects via an individual set of instances. Given that individual projects are rarely treated as islands without any integrated systems, you get to a situation where a coordinated approach for more than just one project needs to be found.

Let's first have a look at what the 6 Rs are and where the concept comes from. Essentially, you can think of each "R" as an available migration strategy for your applications. Each strategy indicates a clear outcome for a transformed application, but not necessarily the actual migration steps to take. The concept was first mentioned by the Gartner analyst Richard Watson (*https://oreil.ly/tk08O*) in 2011. The five original strategies—namely Rehost, Refactor, Revise, Rebuild, and Replace—were revived and adapted in a popular blog post (*https://oreil.ly/CAalp*) by Stephen Orban of AWS in 2016. Orban kept some of Gartner's strategies and added a new one. Thus, the 5 Rs became the 6 Rs. Today, the 6 Rs are used as a fundamental guideline for almost any cloud transformation. Although there are still disputes about whether further strategies should be added, and you can even find 7 Rs, we stick to the 6 Rs in this book as shown in Figure 3-1.

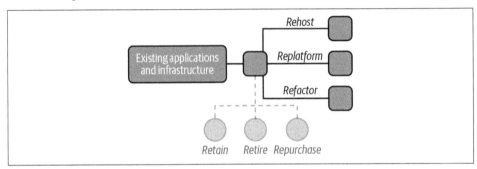

*Figure 3-1. Six modernization approaches, an overview of the 6 Rs*

### Retain—Modernize later or not at all

Everyone has heard the stereotypical story of a mainframe in the basement of some very well-known company, where all of its business secrets are stored. Oftentimes, these mainframes are programmed in CICS (Customer Information Control System, a family of mixed-language application servers that provide online transaction management and connectivity for applications on IBM mainframe systems) and the data is stored in IMS (IBM Information Management System, an early database). And this isn't necessarily a bad thing. Maybe the existing system is a perfect fit for the business and does not need to participate in a modernization project. In order to correctly scope your transformation and modernization efforts, you need to identify those systems and omit them from the modernization process. Systems with this classification need a particular integration approach that needs to be explicitly designed. Imagine a highly scalable mobile application backend that connects directly to a mainframe. In this scenario, the requests from the potentially many mobile devices would overload the costly mainframe. Retain, in this case, does not mean "untouched" but rather "not moved."

### Retire—Turn system off

Some candidates may clearly have reached end-of-life and are already migrated and replaced or just a relic that isn't needed going forward. Travel light and make sure to flag these systems. Subsequent housekeeping is as equally essential as building new things. Investing time to validate and decide on retiring a system is as valuable as a redesign would be.

### Repurchase—Buy new version

In some cases, you can repurchase off-the-shelf software and get it ready made for a new execution environment. That sounds straightforward but will most likely include a migration project and reevaluation of feature lists, mostly because it is unlikely that you can update without changing the product version or its APIs. In some rare cases, you might even find missing integration documentation to be a blocker. This is why it is essential to treat this as a modernization project and not as a simple software update.

### Rehost—Put into containers

Often referred to as "lift and shift," one option for containerizing an application is to simply port the existing architecture as-is to run inside of a container. While this can be as simple as it sounds, there are some challenges on the way. In particular, there can be difficulties when it comes to optimizing the JVM for constrained container runtimes. Some existing middleware application servers come with their vendor-supported base images and make it convenient to switch runtimes. Particular focus should be placed on storage for stateful application runtimes. Java application servers require some data to survive container restarts and require persistent volume mappings. Transactions, load balancing, and in-memory session replication need extended configurations to ensure correct shutdown behavior and node communication. Plan for sufficient research and testing and make sure to adhere to the vendor recommendations. This step is addressing infrastructure modernization and not concerned with application code directly. Existing applications that qualify for such an approach are those that need to move to a container runtime before a refactoring can occur or as an interim step toward switching data center concepts.

 Martin Fowler coined the term "strangler pattern" (*https://oreil.ly/ 0otPb*) as a way to extract functionality out of a monolithic application. It is named after the Australian strangler figs that grow roots from seeds in the upper branches until they touch the ground.

### Replatform—Make some slight adjustments

As an extension to rehosting, replatforming categorizes applications that undergo a conceptual or functional change while switching runtimes. It can also be referred to by its own "lift" name variation, "lift and adjust." It can be related to a strangled functionality, which might be implemented on top of a new technology stack or a change in data storage or integration systems. We recommend using this approach as an initial step toward refactoring and decoupling a monolithic application. Prepending this step leads to smoother operations executing on subsequent extensions and decoupling stages. By choosing to replatform, you are allowing a gentle start to modernizing your applications and pragmatically evolving them.

### Refactor—Build new

Refactoring (*https://refactoring.com*) is a disciplined technique for restructuring an existing body of code, altering its internal structure without changing its external behavior. Refactoring is the most time-consuming and costly way to move existing applications onto a new runtime or platform. It may or may not include a switch to different architecture styles or on-premise or cloud hosting.

# Divide and Containerize

Now that we have looked at different modernization strategies for existing applications, and we know how and when to apply them. It is time to think about other prerequisites for our target platform.

## Kubernetes as the New Application Server?

The word "platform" in the Enterprise Java world normally refers to the application server. Application servers follow a guardrailed software development approach with standardized APIs. The vertical layers are defined by what is commonly refered to as technical layers of a three-tier system. Presentation on top of business on top of data access and/or integration. Horizontally to this we usually find business components or domains. While the vertical layers are usually well separated and decoupled, it is common to find shared classess and violated access rules between the horizontal components. If this happens frequently across the code base, we talk about entangled designs that turn into unmaintainable monoliths over time. But no matter how entangled the application code is, it still profits from the standard application server functionalities addressing nonfunctional and functional requirements like security, isolation, fault tolerance, transaction management, configuration management, etc.

If we fast-forward to distributed architectures of today, where applications consist of many small services, we observe two things: there is no longer a shortcut to a good component design, and the standard application server features are no longer available to our components.

The first observation leads to a mandatory requirement. Distributed services have to be well designed, loosely coupled, and strongly encapsulated components. We will talk more about design principles and approaches for modernizing monoliths in Chapter 5. The second observation holds a list of missing funcionalities in cloud native runtimes. If an application server isn't providing support for commonly used functionalities like we mentioned, there are only two places left. One can be the microservices framework of choice (e.g., Quarkus), and another one could be additional frameworks or products on top of Kubernetes.

Let's take a detailed look at some of the most critical functionalities needed in the following chapters. We call them *microservicilities*. The term refers to a list of cross-cutting concerns that a service must implement apart from the business logic to resolve these concerns as summarized in Figure 3-2.

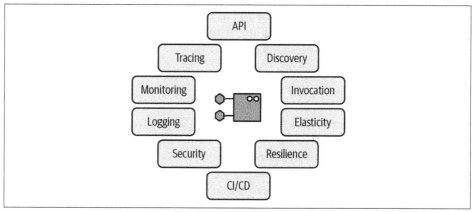

*Figure 3-2. Microservicilities for distributed applications*

### Discovery and configuration

Container images are immutable. Storing configuration options inside them for different environments or stages is discouraged. Instead, the configuration has to be externalized and configured by instance. An externalized configuration is also one of the critical principles of cloud native applications. Service discovery is one way to get configuration information from the runtime environment instead of being hardcoded in the application. Other approaches include using ConfigMaps and Secrets. Kubernetes provides service discovery out of the box, but this might not be sufficient for your application needs. While you can manage the environment settings for each runtime environment through YAML files, additional UIs or CLIs can make it easier for DevOps teams to share responsibility.

### Basic invocation

Applications running inside containers are accessed through Ingress controllers. Ingress exposes HTTP and HTTPS routes from outside the cluster to services within the cluster. Traffic routing is controlled by rules defined on the Ingress resource. Traditionally, this can be compared with Apache HTTP-based load balancers. Other alternatives include projects like HAProxy (*http://www.haproxy.org*) or Nginx. You can use the routing capabilities to do rolling deployments as the basis for a sophisticated CI/CD strategy. For one-time jobs, such as batch processes, Kubernetes provides job and cron-job functionality.

### Elasticity

Kubernetes's ReplicaSets control scaling of pods. It is a way to reconcile a desired state: you tell Kubernetes what state the system should be in so it can figure out how to reach the outcome. A ReplicaSet controls the number of replicas, or exact copies, of a container that should be running at any time. What sounds like a largely static operation can be automated. The Horizontal Pod Autoscaler scales the number of pods based on observed CPU utilization. It is possible to use a custom metric or almost any other application-provided metric as input.

### Logging

One of the more challenging aspects of a distributed application is the correlation of logs from each active part. This is an area where the difference from traditional application servers becomes very visible because it used to be so simple and isn't in the new world. Storing them individually, per container, is not recommended because you lose sight of the bigger picture and have a hard time debugging side effects and root causes for issues. There are various approaches to this, with most of them extensively using the ELK (*https://oreil.ly/XflXI*) (Elasticsearch (*https://oreil.ly/FKoKx*), Logstash (*https://oreil.ly/YLtNc*), Kibana (*https://oreil.ly/h2nIX*)) stack or a variant. In those stacks, Elasticsearch is the object store, where all logs are stored. Logstash gathers logs from nodes and feeds them to Elasticsearch. Kibana is the web UI for Elasticsearch, which is used to search the aggregated log files from various sources.

### Monitoring

Monitoring in a distributed application is an essential ingredient to make sure all of the bits and pieces continue working. In contrast to logging, monitoring is an active observation often paired with alerting rather than simply recording events. Prometheus (*https://prometheus.io*) is the de facto standard for storing the generated information. Essentially, it is a complete open source monitoring system that includes a time-series database. Prometheus's web UI gives you access to metric querying, alerting, and visualizations and helps you gain insights into your systems.

## Build and deployment pipelines

CI/CD (Continuous Integration/Continuous Delivery) isn't anything new to Enterprise Java applications or distributed applications. As a good software development practice, every production code should follow a strict and automated release cycle. With a potentially large number of services that compose an application, the automation should at least aim for 100% coverage. Traditionally a job for the open source tool Jenkins (*https://www.jenkins.io*), modern container platforms have moved away from a centralized build system and embrace a distributed approach to CI/CD. One example is Tekton (*https://tekton.dev*). The goal is to create reliable software releases through build, test, and deployment. We dig deeper into this in Chapter 4.

## Resilience and fault tolerance

Psychologists define "resilience" as the process of adapting well in the face of adversity, trauma, tragedy, threats, or significant sources of stress. In distributed applications, it is the concept of recovering from failure or load scenarios without human interaction. Kubernetes provides resilience options for the cluster itself, but only sparsely supports application resiliency and fault tolerance. For example, application-level resiliency can be facilitated through PersistentVolumes that support replicated volumes or with ReplicaSets ensuring a consistent number of pod replicas across the cluster. On an application level, there is resilience and fault-tolerance support through Istio or various frameworks like Cloudstate (*https://cloudstate.io*). You want to use features such as retry rules, circuit breaker, and pool ejection.

> Istio (*https://istio.io*) is an open source service mesh that layers transparently onto existing distributed applications. It is also a platform, including APIs that integrate into any logging platform, telemetry, or policy system.

## Security

Authentication or Authorization between services is not part of Kubernetes itself. There are two ways to implement it. Using Istio, each service is provided with a strong identity that represents its role and enables interoperability across clusters and clouds. It secures service-to-service communication, as well as providing a key management to automate key and certificate generation, distribution, rotation, and revocation. A more application-centric alternative can be to use a single-sign-on component like Keycloak (*https://www.keycloak.org*) or relying on Eclipse MicroProfile JSON Web Token (*https://oreil.ly/bVETR*) (JWT).

### Tracing

Tracing gives you a way to follow request paths and events throughout the system across individual application parts by still allowing you to trace back to an origin. You can find different approaches across the community today. Independent of languages, frameworks, or technologies you intend to use, Istio can enable distributed tracing. There are other commercial and open source projects available helping with distributed tracing across your application components. Zipkin (*https://zipkin.io*) and Jaeger (*https://www.jaegertracing.io*) are two possible solutions.

## Define Your Target Platform

It's important to note that the nine elements mentioned previously are focused on application development and do not capture all the necessities of a modern container platform. Just looking at this narrow focus leaves important areas unaddressed. A container platform needs to provide features and capabilities for the complete team from Dev to Ops. Depending on specific needs, there is no one-size-fits-all solution. A comprehensive way to define your target platform is to start with the three main layers: Core, Customer Experience, and Integration, then build your application landscape on an optimized technology stack. What sounds like a ready-to-use checklist is anything but. Companies are different in culture, technologies, and requirements, and the following lists are a recommended starting point without any claim to comprehensiveness. We recommend using the bullet points as evaluation categories and defining the individual functional and nonfunctional requirements underneath with a fulfillment score from zero (not available) to three (fully supported) with a middle score of two (can make it work) as a medium evaluation. Finally, add weighting logic to it to reach a complete evaluation based on a product comparison. It can be the core framework for a direct product versus do-it-yourself (DIY) comparison and also the starting point for the platform documentation.

### Define the core

Start with evaluating the core part of the platform. This category includes basic capabilities like container orchestration, storage mapping, rolling upgrades, site reliability engineering (SRE) requirements, out-of-the-box support for the desired deployment models, and might even include further support for virtual machines. This category represents the technical foundation for your target platform:

- Existing core capabilities
- Functional gap assessment
- Hybrid-cloud support
- Security integration

---

- Managed services support
- Operators/marketplace available (e.g., OperatorHub (*https://operatorhub.io*), Red Hat Marketplace (*https://oreil.ly/sFuDg*))
- Available support levels
- Target deployment model
- Core modernization approach

### Define the customer experience layer

When thinking about platforms, one part gets too little attention: the customer experience layer, which contains a technical definition for the customer channels to the platform. A channel can be one of the B2X (business to something) portals or various other specific frontends. A cohesive platform that can host various applications also needs to include a clear definition for the technical composition of the individual services:

- Define customer-centric requirements
- Assess existing cx framework versus build
- Micro frontends (e.g., Entando (*https://dev.entando.org*))
- Integration requirements
- Data gap analysis
- Mobile support

### Define the integration

In a containerized world, integration becomes a new challenge. Coming from a traditional enterprise landscape, it has either been a centralized solution (Enterprise Service Bus or similar) or been part of the individual applications using some common integration framework like Apache Camel. Neither approach fits perfectly into a stateless container-oriented platform. What you are looking for in a target platform is the smooth integration between messaging components, data transformation logic, and service integration. All the relevant parts need to scale well in a stateless environment for distributed systems, and it should be easy to extend a composed application with new capabilities:

- Existing integration capabilities
- Evaluate partner solution ecosystem
- Define integration requirements (data sources, service integration, messaging, APIs)

- Define standards and frameworks (e.g., Camel K (*https://oreil.ly/kfXw1*))
- Evaluate serverless/knative integration (e.g., Camel K)

### Define the technology stack

The remaining category focuses on individual technologies and frameworks. Think of it as a blueprint repository defining the relevant technologies, services, and methodologies for a productive environment. An underestimated influence on the requirements in this category is the available development skill in an organization. With a traditional Enterprise Java background, it is not easy to completely switch to a reactive development approach and a stateless application design. Also, familiarity with existing APIs and time to productivity on a new platform play a crucial role in picking the most suitable technology stack:

- Technology stack assessment across core, CX, and external services
- Microservices framework (e.g, Quarkus, Spring Boot)
- Implementation recommendation (reactive, imperative, message-driven, etc.)
- Deployment model (IaaS, PaaS, hybrid)
- Define target development platform
- Development skills gap analysis

After completing this assessment, you are well prepared for a journey to a containerized application platform. Next, you will need to map out and plan your containerization strategy.

# Mandatory Migration Steps and Tools

Following the basic assumption that you have an existing application landscape in place and cannot start everything as a green-field project, we emphasize moving existing applications into containers. Coming back to the 6 Rs from earlier, the first application you are taking a look at should fall into one of the following Rs: Rehost, Replatform, and Refactor (Figure 3-3). While they look similar in their description, the most significant difference between the three approaches is business value versus migration time and cost.

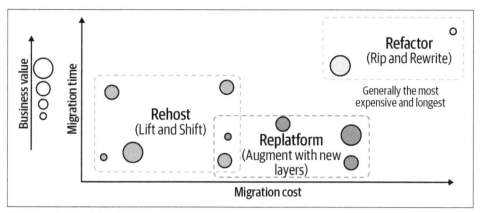

*Figure 3-3. Workload migration pattern*

Which action to take and where to start modernizing depends on the application. While the concrete steps may vary, the first thing to identify is the correct candidates. Therefore, we need to analyze the existing applications, catalog them, and group them to assign them to the final migration pattern. The last step is to execute the individual migration projects.

## Create an Application Portfolio

There are many ways to create such an application catalog or portfolio. And you most likely already have a way to select applications relevant for a certain business domain. If not, feel free to fast-forward to Chapter 5, where we talk about the Konveyor project (*https://oreil.ly/1wPUF*).

# Prepare for Big Things

The most prestigious process in modernization is refactoring existing applications. For coverage of a proven method of transitioning an existing monolithic system to a microservice architecture, we recommend *Monolith to Microservices* (*https://oreil.ly/0x6oq*) by Sam Newman (O'Reilly). While he walks you through a lot of different approaches and creates a detailed process for various situations, there are also simpler approaches, such as the one outlined by Brent Frye from the Software Engineering Institute at Carnegie Mellon University. His approach to modularization (*https://oreil.ly/YKYUY*) of existing applications is a lot more generic. He recommends eight simple steps to break down the monolith. He focuses on components and component groups. *Components* are logical sets of data objects and the actions that the system performs on those objects. Component groups become what he calls *macroservices*. A macroservice is similar to a microservice with two primary differences. First, a macroservice may share the datastore with the legacy monolithic system or other macroservices. Second, unlike a microservice, a macroservice may provide access to multiple data objects. In the last step, the macroservices are decomposed further.

The logical steps to breaking down your monolith according to Frye are:

1. Identify logical components.
2. Flatten and refactor components.
3. Identify component dependencies.
4. Identify component groups.
5. Create an API for a remote user interface.
6. Migrate component groups to macroservices:
   a. Move component groups to separate projects.
   b. Make separate deployments.
7. Migrate macroservices to microservices.
8. Repeat steps 6–7 until complete.

This is also the more general recommendation from Chris Richardson. As he outlined in his O'Reilly SACON London keynote (*https://oreil.ly/CZn61*) and many times after, he is looking for an incremental approach starting with the most promising functionality.

Do it incrementally and repeat the extraction steps until the monolith is finally eliminated or the initial software delivery problems are solved as illustrated in Figure 3-4.

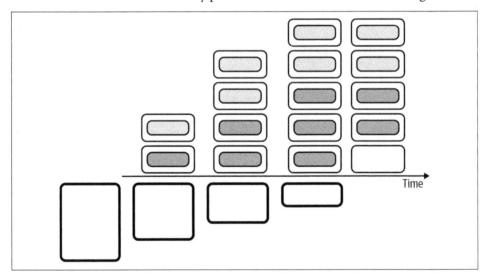

*Figure 3-4. Moving monoliths to services over time by incrementally extracting them*

The three approaches differ in depth, angle, and details. While Richardson talks about the most valuable functionality and focuses on extracting it first, Frye created a simple methodology that can be applied in all situations. Finally, Newman developed the most detailed handbook for various situations in a modernization journey. All three will be helpful on your personal journey. We are convinced, though, that the approach Richardson takes is the best starting point. What Thomas Huijskens said for data scientists is something we also strongly believe in: "The code you write is only useful if it is production code."

Every modernization effort has to follow business requirements and support production functionality. Following this thought, the entire modernization project can only be successful if you identify the correct candidates.

## Summary

This chapter walked you through some basic definitions for migration strategies and showed you an evaluation path for the target development platform. We've looked at technical recommendations, and you now know how to assess existing applications for rehosting, replatforming, and refactoring.

# CHAPTER 4

# A Kubernetes-Based Software Development Platform

In the previous chapter, we outlined our methodology around modernization and the steps required to design and develop modern architectures. We described the need for a platform like Kubernetes that can help you with requirements to make your applications cloud native, ready to scale up proportionally to your business's need.

We have also demonstrated that a microservices-based architecture is usually implemented using container technology, which makes apps portable and consistent. Let's now see in detail how Kubernetes can help us modernize our Java applications and what the steps are to achieve that using its declarative approach through a rich set of APIs.

## Developers and Kubernetes

Kubernetes (*https://kubernetes.io*), which in Greek translates to "pilot" or "governor," is an open source project that is currently the de facto target environment for modern architectures and the most popular container orchestration platform; a simple illustration is presented in Figure 4-1. Started from Google's experience in managing distributed complex applications for their software stack back in 2015, today it is one of the biggest open source communities; it is managed by a foundation, the Cloud Native Computing Foundation (CNCF), and embraced by vendors and individual contributors.

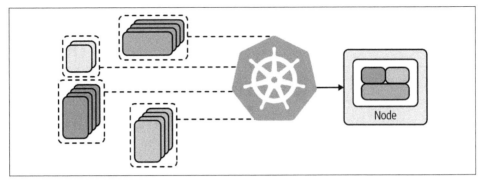

*Figure 4-1. A Kubernetes cluster running apps in Nodes*

As a container-orchestration platform, its focus is primarily on ensuring that our apps are running correctly, providing out-of-the-box self-healing, recovery, and a powerful API to control this mechanism. You may be wondering now: as a developer, why should I care about Kubernetes if it is so self-proficient?

That's a good question, and maybe a good answer is an analogy: you have a Formula 1 car with autopilot, but if you want to win the race, you need to tune and set up your car to compete with all other good ones. The same is true for your apps, which can benefit from all the capabilities offered by the platform to tune them so they run optimally.

## What Kubernetes Does

When you have Kubernetes as a target platform to run your applications, you can rely on an ecosystem of APIs and components put in place to make deployments easier so developers can focus only on the most important part: coding. Kubernetes provides you with a framework to run distributed systems resiliently (*https://oreil.ly/DNRQS*).

In practice, this means you don't need to reimplement custom solutions when it comes to:

*Service discovery*
> Kubernetes uses internal DNS resolution to expose your apps; this is automatically assigned and can also be used to send the traffic to multiple instances of your app.

*Load balancing*
> Kubernetes takes care of managing the load on your apps, balancing the traffic, and distributing user requests accordingly.

*Self-healing*
> Kubernetes discovers and replaces failing containers automatically, providing a health check and self-healing mechanism out of the box.

*Rollout and Rollback*

Kubernetes ensures your app is always running consistently at the desired state, providing control to scale up and scale down workloads. In addition, it offers the capability to rollout or rollback to a specific version of your application.

# What Kubernetes Doesn't Do

Many headaches that developers usually need to deal with in production are already solved and delegated to a platform, whose primary goal is to ensure applications are running. But does that provide all you need for modernizing your apps? Probably not.

As we discussed in the previous chapter, the modernization steps toward a cloud native approach are more closely tied to a methodology rather than a specific technology. Once you've converted your mindset from building monolithic apps to creating microservices, we are in a good position to start thinking big. Nowadays, many apps run on cloud platforms targeting Kubernetes, and those are the ones running global-reach workloads. Here are some things to consider:

- Kubernetes doesn't know how to handle your app. It can restart it if it fails, but it cannot understand why that is happening, so we need to ensure we have full control of our microservices-based architecture and be able to debug each container. This is particularly important in the case of a large-scale deployment.
- Kubernetes doesn't provide any middleware or application-level services. Granular discovery services need to be addressed by interacting with Kubernetes API or relying on some service on top of Kubernetes, such as a service mesh framework. There is no ecosystem for developers out of the box.
- Kubernetes doesn't build your app. You are responsible for providing your app compiled and packaged as a container image or relying on additional components on top of Kubernetes.

With that in mind, let's start digging into a Kubernetes journey for developers in order to make our first step to bringing our app into the next cloud native production environment.

# Infrastructure as a Code

Kubernetes provides a set of APIs to manage the desired state of our app as well as the whole platform. Each component in Kubernetes has an API representation that can be consumed. Kubernetes offers a declarative deployment pattern (*https://oreil.ly/ cURvG*) that allows you to to automate the execution of upgrade and rollback processes for a group of Pods. The declarative approach is granular, and it is also used to extend Kubernetes APIs with the concept of *custom resources*.

Custom resources are extensions of the Kubernetes API. A *custom resource* represents a customization of a particular Kubernetes installation, bringing additional objects to extend cluster capabilities. You can get more info about it from the official Kubernetes documentation (*https://oreil.ly/cVBnl*).

Some of the core objects you have to manage an application in Kubernetes are:

*Pod*
> A group of one or more containers deployed into a Kubernetes cluster. This is the entity that Kubernetes manages and orchestrates, so any application packaged as a container needs to be declared as a Pod.

*Service*
> The resource responsible for service discovery and load balancing. For any Pod to be discoverable and consumable, it needs to be mapped to a Service.

*Deployment*
> This allows describing an application's life cycle, driving the creation of Pods in terms of which images to use for the app, the number of Pods there should be, and how they should be updated. Furthermore, it helps to define health checks and constraint resources for your application.

Each of these objects, along with all other resources in the cluster, can be defined and controlled with a YAML representation, or by Kubernetes API. There are also other useful API objects such as those related to storage (PersistentVolume) or used specifically to manage stateful apps (StatefulSet). In this chapter, we will focus on the fundamental ones needed to bring your app up and running inside a Kubernetes platform.

# Container Images

The first step for you in this journey is to containerize your microservices so they can be deployed into Kubernetes as a Pod, which is controlled by using a YAML file, invoking the API, or using a Kubernetes Java client.

You can use the Inventory Quarkus microservice from Coolstore as an example to create your first container image. Containers are defined by a manifest called Dockerfile or Containerfile, where you will define your software stack as a layer, from the operating system layer to your application binary layer. The benefits of this approach are multiple: it is easy to track versions, inherit from existing layers, add layers, and expand the container. A diagram of layers is shown in Figure 4-2.

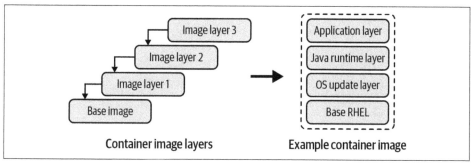

*Figure 4-2. Container image layers*

# Dockerfile

Writing a Dockerfile to package our app as a container is pretty straightforward for simple use cases. There are some basic directives called *Instructions* to use, such as the ones listed in Table 4-1.

*Table 4-1. Dockerfile Instructions*

| Instruction | Description |
| --- | --- |
| FROM | Used to inherit from a base image. For example, it can be a Linux distribution like `fedora`, `centos`, `rhel`, `ubuntu`. |
| ENV | Use environment variable for the container. These variables will be visible to the application and can be set at runtime. |
| RUN | Execute a command in the current layer, like installing a package or executing an application. |
| ADD | Copy files from your workstation to the container layer, like a JAR file or a configuration file. |
| EXPOSE | If your application is listening to some port, you can expose it to the container network so Kubernetes can map it to a Pod and a Service. |
| CMD | The command you use to start your application: the final step of the container image building process where you have all your dependencies in the layers, and you can run your app safely. |

The process for creating your container from your Dockerfile is also described in Figure 4-3.

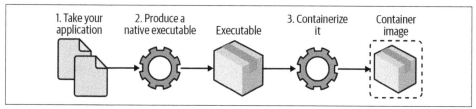

*Figure 4-3. Building a container image*

An example of a Dockerfile for the Inventory Quarkus Java microservice that we created in Chapter 2 is listed next, and you can find it in this book's GitHub repository (*https://oreil.ly/D9u1k*):

```
FROM registry.access.redhat.com/ubi8/openjdk-11 ❶
ENV PROFILE=prod ❷
ADD target/*.jar app.jar ❸
EXPOSE 8080 ❹
CMD java -jar app.jar ❺
```

❶ We start from OpenJDK 11 layer to build our container image.

❷ Set an environment variable that can be consumed within the app for differentiating profiles or configurations to load.

❸ Copy the JAR artifact built during compilation into the container image. This supposes you have compiled a "fat-jar" or "uber-jar" that contains all dependencies in the same JAR file.

❹ Expose port 8080 to the container network.

❺ Run the application invoking the artifact we copied into the layer.

In this section, we defined a Dockerfile with the minimum instructions set to build up a container image. Let's see now how to create container images from a Dockerfile.

## Building Container Images

Now you need to create the container image. Docker (*https://www.docker.com*) is a popular open source project to create containers; you can download it for your operating system and start using it to build and run your containers. Podman (*https://podman.io*) is another open source alternative to do this, and it can also generate Kubernetes objects.

When you have Docker or Podman on your workstation, you can start building your container from the Dockerfile with this command:

```
docker build -f Dockerfile -t docker.io/modernizingjavaappsbook/
    inventory-quarkus:latest
```

This will generate your container image by reading the instructions from the Dockerfile. Then it will tag your container image in the form `<repository>/<name>:<tag>`, in this case, `docker.io/modernizingjavaappsbook/inventory-quarkus:latest`. You will see an output similar to this:

```
STEP 1: FROM registry.access.redhat.com/ubi8/openjdk-11
Getting image source signatures
Copying blob 57562f1b61a7 done
```

```
Copying blob a6b97b4963f5 done
Copying blob 13948a011eec done
Copying config 5d89ab50b9 done
Writing manifest to image destination
Storing signatures
STEP 2: ENV PROFILE=prod
STEP 3: ADD target/*.jar app.jar
STEP 4: EXPOSE 8080
STEP 5: CMD java -jar app.jar
STEP 6: COMMIT inventory-quarkus:latest
Getting image source signatures
Copying blob 3aa55ff7bca1 skipped: already exists
Copying blob 00af10937683 skipped: already exists
Copying blob 7f08faf4d929 skipped: already exists
Copying blob 1ab317e3c719 done
Copying config b2ae304e3c done
Writing manifest to image destination
Storing signatures
--> b2ae304e3c5
b2ae304e3c57216e42b11d8be9941dc8411e98df13076598815d7bc376afb7a1
```

Your container image is now stored in Docker's or Podman's local storage called *Docker cache* or *Container cache*, and it is ready to be used locally.

 You can create an Uber-Jar for production for the Inventory service with this command: `./mvnw package -Dquarkus.profile=prod`. You can let Docker or Podman compile your software and create the container using a particular kind of container images build called Multi-stage (*https://oreil.ly/HzhDj*). See this Dockerfile (*https://oreil.ly/UK3c2*) as an example.

## Run Containers

*Running containers* refers to pulling the container images from the container cache to run applications. This process will be isolated by the container runtime (such as Docker or Podman) from the other ones in our workstation, providing a portable application with all dependencies managed inside a container and not in our workstation.

To start testing the Inventory microservice packaged now as a container image, you can run the command below:

```
docker run -ti docker.io/modernizingjavaappsbook/inventory-quarkus:latest
```

You see that the Quarkus microservice is up and running in a container, listening to the port 8080. Docker or Podman takes care of mapping container networking into your workstation; open your browser at *http://localhost:8080*, and you will see the Quarkus welcome page (as in Figure 2-4).

Docker Network documentation (*https://oreil.ly/ja9Iu*) contains more info on how to map ports and networks within containers and hosts running Docker.

# Registry

As we described in the previous section, container images are stored in a local cache. However, if you want to make them available outside your workstation, you need to send them over in some convenient way. A container image's size is generally hundreds of megabytes. That's why you need a container image registry.

The registry essentially acts as a place to store container images and share them via a process of uploading to (pushing) and downloading from (pulling). Once the image is on another system, the original application contained within it can be run on that system as well.

Registries can be public or private. Popular public registries include Docker Hub (*https://hub.docker.com*) and Quay.io (*https://quay.io*). They are offered as a SaaS on the internet and allow images to be available publicly with or without authentication. Private registries are usually dedicated to specific users and are not accessible for public usage. However, you may make them available to private environments, such as private Kubernetes clusters.

In this example, we created an organization at DockerHub for the book, called `modernizingjavaappsbook`, that maps into a repository of this public registry where we want to push our container image.

First, you need to log in to the registry. You need to authenticate against it in order to be able to push new content, then you will leave the container image publicly available:

```
docker login docker.io
```

After you log in successfully, you can start uploading the Inventory container image to the registry:

```
docker push docker.io/modernizingjavaappsbook/inventory-quarkus:latest
```

This command pushes the images to the registry, and you should get output similar to the following as confirmation:

```
Getting image source signatures
Copying blob 7f08faf4d929 done
Copying blob 1ab317e3c719 done
Copying blob 3aa55ff7bca1 skipped: already exists
Copying blob 00af10937683 skipped: already exists
Copying config b2ae304e3c done
```

```
Writing manifest to image destination
Storing signatures
```

The Quarkus microservice, packaged as a container image, is now ready to be deployed everywhere!

# Deploying to Kubernetes

Deploying applications to Kubernetes is done by interacting with Kubernetes API to create the objects representing the desired state of the app in a Kubernetes cluster. As we discussed, Pods, Services, and Deployments are the minimum objects created to let Kubernetes manage the entire application life cycle and connectivity.

> If you don't have a Kubernetes cluster yet, you can download and use minikube (*https://oreil.ly/n2Kgx*), a standalone Kubernetes cluster designed for local development.

Every object in Kubernetes contains the following values:

*apiVersion*
Kubernetes API version used to create this object

*kind*
The object type (e.g. Pod, Service)

*metadata*
Pieces of information that help uniquely identify the object, such as a name or UID

*spec*
The desired state for the object

In this section, we defined the basic structure of any Kubernetes objects. Now, let's explore the fundamental objects needed to run applications on top of Kubernetes.

# Pod

A Pod (*https://oreil.ly/KQk2T*) is a group of one or more containers with shared storage and network resources and a specification for how to run the containers. In Figure 4-4, you can see a representation of two Pods in a Kubernetes cluster, with an example IP address assigned by Kubernetes to each of them.

*Figure 4-4. Pods and containers*

Kubernetes doesn't work directly with containers; it relies on the Pod concept to orchestrate containers. As such, you need to provide a Pod definition that matches your container:

```
apiVersion: v1
kind: Pod
metadata:
  name: inventory-quarkus ❶
  labels:
    app: inventory-quarkus ❷
spec:
  containers: ❸
    - name: inventory-quarkus
      image: docker.io/modernizingjavaappsbook/inventory-quarkus:latest ❹
      ports:
        - containerPort: 8080 ❺
```

❶ Name for the Pod object, unique per Namespace

❷ A list of key/value pairs to apply to this object

❸ A list of containers used in this Pod

❹ The container image URI, in this case a repository publicly available in Docker Hub

❺ The port exposed by this container, to be mapped into a Pod

 Generally, one Pod contains one container, thus the mapping is 1 Pod : 1 application. Although you could have multiple containers in one Pod for some use cases (e.g., sidecars), the best practice is to map 1 Pod to 1 app, because this ensures scalability and maintainability.

You can create any of the Kubernetes objects described previously as a YAML file with the Kubernetes CLI kubectl. Run the command as shown next to deploy your first microservice as a single Pod. You can find it in this book's GitHub repository (*https://oreil.ly/YF8bT*):

```
kubectl create -f pod.yaml
```

To check that it is running on Kubernetes:

```
kubectl get pods
```

You should get an output similar to:

```
NAME                 READY  STATUS   RESTARTS  AGE
inventory-quarkus    1/1    Running  0         30s
```

If you look at the STATUS column, it shows the Pod is running correctly and all default health checks are correctly satisfied.

 If you want further details on how to make more granular health checks, please refer to the official Kubernetes documentation for liveness and readiness probes (*https://oreil.ly/sOdnL*).

## Service

Kubernetes Services (*https://oreil.ly/fOfpN*) are used to expose an application running on a set of Pods. This is useful because a Pod gets a random IP address from the Kubernetes network, which may change if it is restarted or moved to another node within a Kubernetes cluster. Services offers a more consistent way to communicate with Pods, acting as a DNS server and load balancer.

A Service is mapped to one or more Pods; it uses the internal DNS to resolve to an internal IP from a mnemonic short hostname (e.g., inventory-quarkus), and balances the traffic to the Pods as shown in Figure 4-5. Each Service get its own IP address from a dedicated IP address range, which is different from a Pod's IP address range.

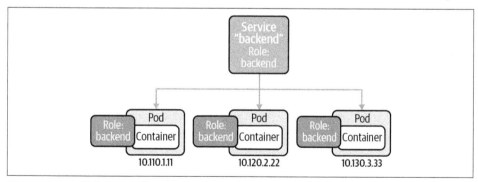

*Figure 4-5. A Kubernetes Service*

The balancing method offered by Kubernetes Services is Layer 4 (TCP/UDP). The only two strategies usable are round-robin and source IP. For application layer balancing (e.g., HTTP), there are other objects like `Ingress` not covered in this book, but you can find the documentation for them here (*https://oreil.ly/VBvOu*).

Let's have a look at a Service that could map our Pod:

```yaml
apiVersion: v1
kind: Service
metadata:
  name: inventory-quarkus-service ❶
spec:
  selector:
    app: inventory-quarkus ❷
  ports:
    - protocol: TCP ❸
      port: 8080 ❹
      targetPort: 8080 ❺
```

❶ Name for the Service object

❷ The label exposed by the Pod to match the Service

❸ The L4 protocol used, TCP or UDP

❹ The port used by this Service

❺ The port used by the Pod and mapped into the Service

To create your Service, run the command as shown below. You can also find it in this book's GitHub repository (*https://oreil.ly/e13Dd*):

```
kubectl create -f service.yaml
```

To check that it is running on Kubernetes:

```
kubectl get svc
```

You should get output similar to:

```
NAME                        TYPE       CLUSTER-IP     EXTERNAL-IP  PORT(S)   AGE
inventory-quarkus-service   ClusterIP  172.30.34.73   <none>       8080/TCP  6s
```

You just defined a Service, mapped to a Pod. This is only accessible from the internal Kubernetes network, unless you expose it with an object that can accept the traffic from outside the cluster, like Ingress.

# Deployment

Deployments are Kubernetes objects created for managing an application life cycle. A deployment describes a desired state, and Kubernetes will implement it using either a *rolling* or *re-create* deployment strategy. The rollout life cycle consists of progressing, complete, and failed states. A deployment is progressing while it is performing update tasks, such as updating or scaling Pods.

Kubernetes deployments offer a set of capabilities on top of the basic Pod and Service concepts as listed next and in Figure 4-6:

- Deploy a ReplicaSet or Pod
- Update Pods and ReplicaSets
- Rollback to previous deployment versions
- Scale a deployment
- Pause or continue a deployment
- Define health checks
- Define resources constraints

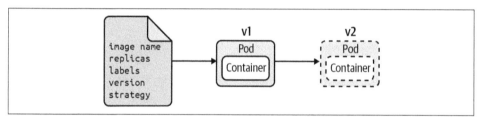

*Figure 4-6. Deployments manage an application's life cycle and updates*

Managing applications with a Kubernetes deployment includes the way in which an application should be updated. A major benefit of a deployment is the ability to start and stop a set of Pods predictably. There are two strategies for deploying apps in Kubernetes:

*Rolling update*
It provides a controlled, phased replacement of the application's Pods, ensuring that there are always a minimum number available. This is useful for the business continuity of an application, where the traffic is not routed into a new version of the application until the health checks (probes) on the desired number of Pods deployed are satisfied.

*Re-create*

It removes all existing pods before new ones are created. Kubernetes first termi-
nates all containers from the current version and then starts all new containers
simultaneously when the old containers are gone. This provides downtime for
the app, but it ensures there aren't multiple versions running at the same time.

A `Deployment` object driving Pods deployment on Kubernetes is listed in the following example:

```
apiVersion: apps/v1
kind: Deployment
metadata:
  name: inventory-quarkus-deploy ❶
  labels:
    app: inventory-quarkus ❷
spec:
  replicas: 1 ❸
  selector:
    matchLabels:
      app: inventory-quarkus ❹
  template: ❺
    metadata:
      labels:
        app: inventory-quarkus
    spec:
      containers:
      - name: inventory-quarkus
        image: docker.io/modernizingjavaappsbook/inventory-quarkus:latest ❻
        ports:
        - containerPort: 8080
        readinessProbe: ❼
          httpGet:
            path: /
            port: 8080
            scheme: HTTP
          periodSeconds: 10
          successThreshold: 1
          failureThreshold: 3
        livenessProbe: ❽
          httpGet:
            path: /
            port: 8080
            scheme: HTTP
          periodSeconds: 10
          successThreshold: 1
          failureThreshold: 3
```

❶   Name for the Deployment object.

❷   The label for this object.

❸ The desired number of Pod replicas.

❹ The selector to find which Pods to manage using labels.

❺ The Pod template to use, including labels to inherit or containers to create.

❻ The container image to use.

❼ Kubernetes uses readiness probes to know when a container is ready to start accepting traffic, and a Pod is considered ready when all of its containers are ready. Here we define an HTTP health check on the root path as a readiness probe.

❽ Kubernetes uses liveness probes to know when to restart a container. Here we define an HTTP health check on the root path as a liveness probe.

Run the following command to create your Deployment. You can also find it in this book's GitHub repository (*https://oreil.ly/PWucG*):

```
kubectl create -f deployment.yaml
```

Run the following command to verify that the Deployment has been created, and to get the status:

```
kubectl get deploy
```

You should get output similar to:

```
NAME                      READY   UP-TO-DATE   AVAILABLE   AGE
inventory-quarkus-deploy  1/1     1            1           10s
```

Looking at the READY column, you have your desired state correctly matched, having requested one replica for the Inventory microservice running on Kubernetes. You can cross-check that a Pod has been created:

```
kubectl get pods
```

You should get similar output to:

```
NAME                                        READY   STATUS    RESTARTS   AGE
inventory-quarkus                           1/1     Running   0          1m
inventory-quarkus-deploy-5cb46f5d8d-fskpd   1/1     Running   0          30s
```

Now a new Pod has been created using a randomly generated name, starting from the inventory-quarkus-deploy Deployment name. If the app crashes or if we kill the Pod managed by the Deployment, Kubernetes will re-create it automatically for us. This is not true for the Pod generated without a Deployment:

```
kubectl delete pod inventory-quarkus inventory-quarkus-deploy-5cb46f5d8d-fskpd
```

You can see that the desired state is always met:

```
kubectl get pods
```

You should get output similar to:

```
NAME                                       READY   STATUS    RESTARTS   AGE
inventory-quarkus-deploy-5cb46f5d8d-llp7n  1/1     Running   0          42s
```

# Kubernetes and Java

Kubernetes has a tremendous amount of potential for managing applications' life cycles, and there are a number of studies on how developers and architects could best fit in its architecture, like patterns. Kubernetes patterns are reusable design patterns for container-based applications and services.

From a Java developer perspective, the first step is to migrate from the monolithic approach to a microservice-based approach. Once that is complete, the next step is to get into the Kubernetes context and maximize the benefits this platform offers: API extendibility, a declarative model, and a standarized process where the IT industry is converging.

There are Java frameworks that help developers connect to Kubernetes and convert their apps to containers. You already containerized the Inventory Quarkus microservice with a Dockerfile. Now let's drive this containerization from Java, generating a container image for the Catalog Spring Boot microservice using Maven and Gradle.

## Jib

Jib (*https://oreil.ly/N2jRr*) is an open source framework made by Google to build container images compliant to the Open Container Initiative (OCI) image format, without the need of Docker or any container runtime. You can create containers even from your Java codebase because it offers a Maven and Gradle plug-in for that. This means Java developers can containerize their app without writing and/or maintaining any Dockerfiles, delegating this complexity to Jib.

We see the benefits from this approach (*https://oreil.ly/2y92D*) as follows:

*Pure Java*
No Docker or Dockerfile knowledge is required; simply add Jib as a plug-in, and it will generate the container image for you. The resulting image is commonly referred to as "distroless," since it doesn't inherit from any base image.

*Speed*
The application is divided into multiple layers, splitting dependencies from classes. There's no need to rebuild the container image as is necessary for Dockerfiles; Jib takes care of deploying the layers that changed.

*Reproducibility*

Unnecessary updates are not triggered, as the same contents always generate the same image.

The easiest way to kick-start a container image build with Jib, on existing Maven, is by adding the plug-in via command line:

```
mvn compile com.google.cloud.tools:jib-maven-plugin:2.8.0:build
  -Dimage=<MY IMAGE>
```

Alternatively, you can do so by adding Jib as a plug-in into *pom.xml*:

```
<project>
  ...
  <build>
    <plugins>
      ...
      <plugin>
        <groupId>com.google.cloud.tools</groupId>
        <artifactId>jib-maven-plugin</artifactId>
        <version>2.8.0</version>
        <configuration>
          <to>
            <image>myimage</image>
          </to>
        </configuration>
      </plugin>
      ...
    </plugins>
  </build>
  ...
</project>
```

In this way you can also manage other settings such as authentication or parameters for the build. Run the command below if you want to build the Catalog service and push it directly to Docker Hub:

```
mvn compile com.google.cloud.tools:jib-maven-plugin:2.8.0:build↳
-Dimage=docker.io/modernizingjavaappsbook/catalog-spring-boot:latest↳
-Djib.to.auth.username=<USERNAME>↳
-Djib.to.auth.password=<PASSWORD>
```

The authentication here is managed as command line options, but Jib is able to manage existing authentication with Docker CLI or read credentials from your *settings.xml*.

The build takes a few moments, and the result is a distroless container image built locally and pushed directly to a registry, in this case Docker Hub:

```
[INFO] Scanning for projects...
[INFO]
[INFO] ------------------< com.redhat.cloudnative:catalog >------------------
[INFO] Building CoolStore Catalog Service 1.0-SNAPSHOT
```

```
[INFO] -------------------------------[ jar ]---------------------------------
[INFO]
[INFO] --- maven-resources-plugin:2.6:resources (default-resources) @ catalog ---
[INFO] Copying 4 resources
[INFO]
[INFO] --- maven-compiler-plugin:3.6.1:compile (default-compile) @ catalog ---
[INFO] Nothing to compile - all classes are up to date
[INFO]
[INFO] --- jib-maven-plugin:2.8.0:build (default-cli) @ catalog ---
[INFO]
[INFO] Containerizing application to modernizingjavaappsbook/catalog-spring-boot
    ...
[WARNING] Base image 'gcr.io/distroless/java:11' does not use a specific image
    digest↳ - build may not be reproducible
[INFO] Using credentials from <to><auth> for modernizingjavaappsbook/
    catalog-spring-boot
[INFO] Using base image with digest:↳
sha256:65aa73135827584754f1f1949c59c3e49f1fed6c35a918fadba8b4638ebc9c5d
[INFO]
[INFO] Container entrypoint set to [java, -cp, /app/resources:/app/classes:/app/
    libs/*, com.redhat.cloudnative.catalog.CatalogApplication]
[INFO]
[INFO] Built and pushed image as modernizingjavaappsbook/catalog-spring-boot
[INFO] Executing tasks:
[INFO] [==============================] 100,0% complete
[INFO]
[INFO] ---------------------------------------------------------------------
[INFO] BUILD SUCCESS
[INFO] ---------------------------------------------------------------------
[INFO] Total time:  27.817 s
[INFO] Finished at: 2021-03-19T11:48:16+01:00
[INFO] ---------------------------------------------------------------------
```

Your container image is not present in your local cache, as you don't need any container runtime to build images with Jib. You won't see it with the docker images command, but you pull it from Docker Hub afterward and it will be stored in your cache. In case you also want to store it locally from the beginning, Jib also connects to Docker hosts and can do it for you.

# JKube

Eclipse JKube (*https://oreil.ly/Km2ci*), a community project supported by the Eclipse Foundation and Red Hat, is another open source Java framework to help with interacting with Kubernetes from a Java developer perspective. It supports building container images using Docker/Podman, Jib, and Source-to-Image (S2I). Eclipse JKube also provides a set of tools to deploy automatically to Kubernetes and manage the application with helpers for debugging and logging. It comes from Fabric8 Maven Plug-in, rebranded and enhanced as a project to target Kubernetes.

JKube supports Kubernetes and OpenShift. OpenShift brings Source-to-Image (*https://oreil.ly/4z2Zn*) on top of Kubernetes, a mechanism to automatically compile a container image from source code. In this way the build is made on Kubernetes, so developers can test and deploy their apps directly on the target platform.

As with Jib, JKube provides Zero Configuration mode for a quick ramp-up where opinionated defaults will be preselected. It provides Inline Configuration within the plug-in configuration using an XML syntax. Furthermore, it provides External Configuration templates of real deployment descriptors, which are enriched by the plug-in.

JKube is offered in three forms:

*Kubernetes Plug-in*
It works in any Kubernetes cluster, providing either distroless or Dockerfile-driven builds.

*OpenShift Plug-in*
It works in any Kubernetes or OpenShift cluster, providing either distroless, Dockerfile-driven builds, or Source-to-Image (S2I) builds.

*JKube Kit*
A toolkit and a CLI to interact with JKube Core, it also acts as a Kubernetes Client and provides an Enricher API to extend Kubernetes manifests.

JKube offers more functionality than Jib; in fact, it can be considered a superset. You can do distroless Jib builds, but you can also work with Dockerfile and deploy Kubernetes manifests from Java. In this case, we don't need to write a Deployment or Service; JKube will take care of building the container and deploy it to Kubernetes.

Let's include JKube in our Catalog POM file and configure it to do a Jib build and a deploy to Kubernetes. Doing so will make the plug-in persistent. You can also find the source code in this book's GitHub repository (*https://oreil.ly/Ba4Ro*).

First, we need to add JKube as a plug-in:

```
<project>
  ...
  <build>
    <plugins>
      ...
      <plugin>
        <groupId>org.eclipse.jkube</groupId>
        <artifactId>kubernetes-maven-plugin</artifactId>
        <version>1.1.1</version>
      </plugin>
      ...
    </plugins>
```

```
    </build>
    ...
  </project>
```

After that, you can drive the container image build with properties. In this case, you may want to use Jib for building the image and pushing it to Docker Hub. Afterward, you will deploy it to Kubernetes:

```
...
<properties>
    ...
    <jkube.build.strategy>jib</jkube.build.strategy>
    <jkube.generator.name>docker.io/modernizingjavaappsbook/catalog-spring-boot:
      ${project.version}</jkube.generator.name>
</properties>
...
```

Let's build the image:

```
mvn k8s:build
```

You should get output similar to:

```
JIB>... modernizingjavaappsbook/catalog-spring-boot/1.0-SNAPSHOT/build/
  deployments/catalog-1.0-SNAPSHOT.jar
JIB>     :
JIB>... modernizingjavaappsbook/catalog-spring-boot/1.0-SNAPSHOT/build/Dockerfile
...
JIB> [========================     ] 80,0% complete > building image to tar file
JIB> Building image to tar file...
JIB> [========================     ] 80,0% complete > writing to tar file
JIB> [=============================] 100,0% complete
[INFO] k8s: ... modernizingjavaappsbook/catalog-spring-boot/1.0-SNAPSHOT/tmp/↳
docker-build.tar successfully built
[INFO] ------------------------------------------------------------------------
[INFO] BUILD SUCCESS
[INFO] ------------------------------------------------------------------------
[INFO] Total time:  36.229 s
[INFO] Finished at: 2021-03-19T13:03:19+01:00
[INFO] ------------------------------------------------------------------------
```

JKube using Jib created the container image locally, and it is now ready to be pushed to Docker Hub. You can specify credentials in one of three ways:

*Docker login*
    You can log in to your registry, in this case Docker Hub, and JKube will read the *~/.docker/config.json* file to get authentication details.

*Provide credentials inside POM*
    Provide registry credentials as part of XML configuration.

*Provide credentials inside Maven Settings*

You can provide registry credentials in your *~/.m2/settings.xml* file and the plug-in will read it from there.

In this case, you use the third option and set up credentials into Maven Settings, so you can copy this file using your credentials. You can also find the source code in this book's GitHub repository (*https://oreil.ly/uxAxW*):

```xml
<?xml version="1.0" encoding="UTF-8"?>
<settings xmlns="http://maven.apache.org/SETTINGS/1.0.0"
          xmlns:xsi="http://www.w3.org/2001/XMLSchema-instance"
          xsi:schemaLocation="http://maven.apache.org/SETTINGS/1.0.0↳
          http://maven.apache.org/xsd/settings-1.0.0.xsd">

  <servers>
    <server>
      <id>https://index.docker.io/v1</id>
      <username>USERNAME</username>
      <password>PASSWORD</password>
    </server>
  </servers>
</settings>
```

To push it to Docker Hub, you just run this Maven goal:

```
mvn k8s:push
```

You should see output similar to:

```
JIB> [=========================] 81,8% complete > scheduling pushing manifests
JIB> [=========================] 81,8% complete > launching manifest pushers
JIB> [=========================] 81,8% complete > pushing manifest for latest
JIB> Pushing manifest for latest...
JIB> [=========================] 90,9% complete > building images to registry
JIB> [=========================] 90,9% complete > launching manifest list pushers
JIB> [=========================] 100,0% complete
[INFO] ------------------------------------------------------------------------
[INFO] BUILD SUCCESS
[INFO] ------------------------------------------------------------------------
[INFO] Total time:  01:08 min
[INFO] Finished at: 2021-03-19T13:21:28+01:00
```

Now it's time to deploy the Catalog on Kubernetes. JKube will connect to your Kubernetes cluster reading the `~/.kube/config` file on your workstation:

```
mvn k8s:resource k8s:apply
```

You should get output similar to:

```
[INFO] Scanning for projects...
[INFO]
[INFO] ------------------< com.redhat.cloudnative:catalog >-------------------
[INFO] Building CoolStore Catalog Service 1.0-SNAPSHOT
[INFO] --------------------------------[ jar ]--------------------------------
```

```
[INFO]
[INFO] --- kubernetes-maven-plugin:1.1.1:resource (default-cli) @ catalog ---
[INFO] k8s: Running generator spring-boot
    ...
[INFO] k8s: Creating a Service from kubernetes.yml namespace default name catalog
[INFO] k8s: Created Service: target/jkube/applyJson/default/service-catalog.json
[INFO] k8s: Creating a Deployment from kubernetes.yml namespace default name
    catalog
[INFO] k8s: Created Deployment: target/jkube/applyJson/default/deployment-
    catalog.json
[INFO] k8s: HINT: Use the command `kubectl get pods -w` to watch your pods start
    up
[INFO] -------------------------------------------------------------------------
[INFO] BUILD SUCCESS
[INFO] -------------------------------------------------------------------------
[INFO] Total time:  7.464 s
[INFO] Finished at: 2021-03-19T13:38:27+01:00
[INFO] -------------------------------------------------------------------------
```

The app has been deployed successfully to Kubernetes, using generated manifests:

```
kubectl get pods

NAME                        READY   STATUS    RESTARTS   AGE
catalog-64869588f6-fpjj8    1/1     Running   0          2m2s

kubectl get deploy

NAME      READY   UP-TO-DATE   AVAILABLE   AGE
catalog   1/1     1            1           3m54s
```

To test it, let's have a look at the Service:

```
kubectl get svc

NAME      TYPE        CLUSTER-IP    EXTERNAL-IP   PORT(S)    AGE
catalog   ClusterIP   10.99.26.127  <none>        8080/TCP   4m44s
```

 By default, Kubernetes exposes the application only internally to the cluster, using `ClusterIP` Service type. You can expose it externally using a Service type `NodePort` or using an Ingress. In this example, you will use `kubectl port-forward` to map the Kubernetes exposed port to our workstation's port.

Let's try our app using the `kubectl port-forward` command:

```
kubectl port-forward deployment/catalog 8080:8080
```

If you open your browser now at *http://localhost:8080/api/catalog*, you will see the Coolstore's Catalog JSON output.

# Summary

In this chapter, we discussed how Java developers can benefit from Kubernetes capabilities to modernize and enhance their apps, showing a developer's inner loop with Kubernetes environments. We have demonstrated how to create container images and how to deploy them to Kubernetes. We also walked through steps to drive container creation and deploy directly from Java with Maven thanks to Jib and JKube.

Modernization is important for developers in order to make apps cloud native and portable, ready for serving highly available productions and services. In the next chapter, we will look deeper into the modernization of existing Java applications and what steps are needed to achieve it.

# CHAPTER 5

# Beyond Lift and Shift: Working with Legacy

Legacy is not what I did for myself. It's what I'm doing for the next generation.

—Vitor Belfort

Many organizations are faced with the challenge of keeping their existing business operations running while also trying to innovate. There are typically increased expectations to deliver new functionality faster and to reduce cost, something that seems challenging when looking at the existing application landscape and prevalence of legacy systems.

We often use the term "legacy system" to describe an old methodology, or technology, or application that is not written according to the latest methods or uses an outdated technology stack. Admittedly, many of the systems we created early on in our career belong to this category. We do know that most of them are still in use. Some of them even paved the way for new approaches or even standards that followed them. We usually also imply that those systems would need a replacement, which ultimately contributes to the perceived negative connotation. Thankfully, this isn't always true. Legacy also is a beautiful word to describe achievements and heritage. Calling something "legacy" doesn't automatically make it outdated and unusable. There are plenty of reasons to keep the legacy systems in place, including:

- The system works as designed, and there is no need to change.
- The business processes implemented are no longer known or documented, and replacing them is expensive.
- The cost for replacing a system is higher than the benefit of keeping it unchanged.

The book *Working Effectively with Legacy Code* (*https://oreil.ly/iogGC*) by Michael Feathers (O'Reilly) provides programmers with techniques to cost-effectively handle common legacy code problems without having to go through the hugely expensive task of rewriting all existing code.

Feathers said, "To me, legacy code is simply code without tests." If we read the term "legacy" today, it primarily refers to monolithic applications. There are various approaches to handling legacy applications in a modern enterprise landscape, and picking the right one is the first and most crucial part of the modernization journey.

We've only talked about individual systems so far. And developers usually only care about this specific system scope. Modernization plans should follow overarching company goals and should also take the company-wide IT strategy into account. A particularly exciting approach for cloud migration is presented in Gregor Hohpe's book *Cloud Strategy: A Decision-Based Approach to Successful Cloud Migration* (*https://oreil.ly/EuW9J*). It is a must-read if you want to know more about building the abstraction above individual migration efforts.

# Managing Legacy

Every successful journey begins with a first step. The first step for an application migration journey is the assessment of the existing applications. We assume that you know the company-wide goals and directives. We can map them into assessment categories now. Another source for assessment categories is technical requirements—for example, existing blueprints or recommended master solutions or framework versions. Building and updating this list of assessment categories should be a recurring task that becomes part of your governance process. Ultimately, you can derive migration criteria from these assessment criteria and use them as decision-making cornerstones for your modernization journey.

## Assessing Applications for Migration

When assessing a migration or modernization effort, it is essential to consider the specific challenges that motivate or influence your organization. Some examples of challenges that organizations might face include:

*Limited budgets for development*
> Development teams need to become more efficient, and their velocity has to increase. Instead of working with complex specifications, they aim to switch to lightweight frameworks and prebuilt functionalities. Modernizations should be usually scheduled as part of an ongoing development or maintanance project.

*Lack of in-house skills*
> The team skills for existing in-house technologies are decreasing. Examples of this are host programming or even earlier versions of Enterprise Java specifications that are no longer taught or state-of-the-art. Changing existing systems that

use older technologies might mean needing to add specific skills for the development project.

*Perceived risks*

Following a famous proverb popularized around 1977, "If it ain't broken, don't fix it," we do see a lot of perceived risks to changing well-established and running software. The reasons for this can be numerous and range from knowledge issues about the system to fear of stopped production in factories. These risks need to be addressed individually and mitigated through suitable actions in the migration plan.

*No known predictable process*

This book helps you with this particular point. Navigating the unknown can be a considerable challenge. Having a proven and repeatable process for modernization efforts in place that all parties respect and follow is critical for success.

*Real effort estimation*

Estimating migration efforts should not be magic. Unfortunately, many companies have a minimal idea about the genuine efforts to modernize Enterprise Java applications. Following a predictable and optimized approach will remove this challenge.

Turning these challenges into actionable items for your assessment can look like this:

- Predicting the level of effort and cost
- Scheduling application migrations and handling conflicts
- Identifying all potential risks at a code, infrastructure, process, or knowledge level
- Predicting the return on investment to make the business case
- Identifying and mitigating risks to the business
- Minimizing disruption to existing business operations

It is sufficient to do this in a spreadsheet or document if you are only looking at a single application. However, every mid- to large-scale effort needs a better solution. Large-scale efforts need automated routines and rules to assess an install base and link applications to business services to plan the next steps reliably. An open source and straightforward way of gathering and managing all relevant information comes from the Konveyor project (*https://www.konveyor.io*). It combines a set of tools that aim at helping with modernization and migration onto Kubernetes.

The Konveyor subproject Forklift provides the ability to migrate virtual machines to KubeVirt with minimal downtime. The subproject Crane concentrates on migrating applications between Kubernetes clusters. Also part of the suite is Move2Kube to help accelerate the replatforming of Swarm and Cloud Foundry-based applications to Kubernetes.

For application modernization in particular, Konveyor offers the Tackle (*https:// oreil.ly/u99Gf*) project. It assesses and analyzes applications for refactoring into containers and provides a standard inventory.

### Tackle Application Inventory

This allows users to maintain their portfolio of applications, link them to the business services they support, and define their interdependencies. The Application Inventory uses an extensible tagging model to add metadata, which is a great way to link migration categories, as discussed earlier. The Application Inventory is used to select an application for an assessment by Pathfinder.

### Tackle Pathfinder

This is an interactive, questionnaire-based tool that assesses the suitability of applications for modernization so they can be deployed in containers on an enterprise Kubernetes platform. Pathfinder (*https://oreil.ly/K4V4u*) generates reports about an application's suitability for Kubernetes, including the associated risk, and creates an adoption plan. Pathfinder does this based on the information present in the application inventory and additional assessment questions. If an application depends on a direct host system connection, it might disqualify this particular application for a migration to Kubernetes because it would overload the host parts. Some examples of assessment questions are:

- Are third-party vendor components supported in containers?
- Is the application under active development?
- Does the application have any legal requirements (e.g., PCI, HIPAA)?
- Does the application provide metrics?

We strongly recommend looking at Pathfinder to manage large-scale modernization projects across complete landscapes. It will help you categorize and prioritize applications in your scope today and continuously track your migration assessment for future changes.

### Tackle Controls

Controls are a collection of entities that add different values to the Application Inventory and the Pathfinder assessment. They comprise business services, stakeholders, stakeholder groups, job functions, tag types, and tags. In addition, you can capture company- or project-specific attributes by implementing your own entities. This will filter your Application Inventory, for example, all applications used by a certain "job function" to identify all applications used by the human resources department.

## Tackle DiVA

Finally, DiVA (*https://oreil.ly/UGzn2*) is a data-centric application analysis tool. As a successor to the project Windup (*https://oreil.ly/sjiNq*), it is the most exciting project to look at if you want to assess individual applications. It focuses on the traditional monolithic application and currently supports Servlets and Spring Boot applications. You can import a set of application source files (Java/XML), and DiVA then provides the following:

- Service entry (exported API) inventory
- Database inventory
- Transaction inventory
- Code-to-Database dependencies (call graphs)
- Database-to-Database dependencies
- Transaction-to-Transaction dependencies
- Transaction refactoring recommendations

DiVA is currently under active development, and the incorporation of the original Windup project isn't finished yet. However, it still gives you a solid foundation for your modernization efforts. Additionally, it presents an excellent opportunity to contribute your findings and become part of a larger community dedicated to automating migrations.

## Migration Toolkit for Applications

While we wait for Windup to be fully integrated into DiVA, you can still use an automated migration assessment for Enterprise Java-based applications by using the Migration Toolkit for Applications (MTA) (*https://oreil.ly/SIOSR*).

MTA assembles tools that support large-scale Enterprise Java application modernization and migration projects across many transformations and use cases. You can import your application binary or archives into it, and it automatically performs code analysis, including the application portfolio, application dependencies, migration challenges, and migration effort estimation in the form of story points. Initially it was designed to support Java EE server migrations (e.g., WebSphere or WebLogic to JBoss EAP). Still, it has a highly extensible rule set mechanism that allows developers to create their own set of rules or even adapt existing ones to their needs. Today it also covers Spring Boot to Quarkus migrations.

An excerpt from an example rule in Java looks like this:

```
//...
JavaClass.references("weblogic.servlet.annotation.WLServlet")
    .at(TypeReferenceLocation.ANNOTATION)
        )
        .perform(
            Classification.as("WebLogic @WLServlet")
                .with(Link.to("Java EE 6 @WebServlet",
                            "https://some.url/index.html"))
                .withEffort(0)
                .and(Hint.withText("Migrate to Java EE 6 @WebServlet."))
                .withEffort(8))
        );
//...
```

This rule scans Java classes for @WLServlet annotations and adds an effort (story points) to this finding. You can learn more about rules and how to develop them in the Windup documentation (*https://oreil.ly/FbQKL*).

Beyond that, it can also support nonmigration use cases as part of a build process (via a Maven plug-in (*https://oreil.ly/T8mom*) or a Command Line Interface (*https:// oreil.ly/U7Dsk*)), either validating code regularly against organizational standards or ensuring application portability.

Some of the patterns MTA can detect include the following:

- Proprietary libraries
- Proprietary configurations
- Service locators
- Web services
- EJB descriptors
- Deprecated Java code
- Transaction managers
- Injection frameworks
- Thread pooling mechanisms
- Timer services
- WAR/EAR descriptors
- Static IP addresses

MTA and DiVA are two potent tools that help us identify overall technical debt, resulting in a classification of migration needs and risks. However, they do not allow us to identify the functionality that should be migrated or modernized first. For this, we need to take a deeper look into the application design and functionality.

# Assessing Functionality for Migration

Traditional monoliths come in various shapes, forms, and sizes. When someone uses the term "monolith," they are usually referring to the deployment artifact itself. In Enterprise Java, this has traditionally been Enterprise Archives (EAR) or Web Archives (WAR). You can also look at them as single-process applications. They can be designed following modularity recommendations like OSGi (Open Services Gateway Initiative) or following more technical approaches like the three-tier design without significant business modules. The overall direction of your modernization efforts heavily depends on the type of monolith you are dealing with. As a rule of thumb, the more modular an existing application already is, the easier it is to modernize it. In a perfect world, modules directly translate into service boundaries. But this rarely happens.

If the monolith seems like a giant box, we have to apply a logical model to it. And we realize that inside this box are organized business and technical components, for example, order management, PDF rendering, client notifications, etc. While the code is probably not organized around these concepts, they exist in the codebase from a business-domain-model perspective. These business domain boundaries, often called "bounded contexts" in Domain-Driven-Design (DDD), become the new services.

If you are interested in learning more, many consider Eric Evans's book *Domain-Driven Design: Tackling Complexity in the Heart of Software* (O'Reilly) (*https://oreil.ly/kgLPl*) the de facto standard introduction to DDD.

Once you have identified the modules and functionality, you can start to think about your modernizing order. But first, make sure to look at the cost versus benefit trade-offs for each module and start with the best candidate. Figure 5-1 gives a very high-level overview of how this could look for a sample application with six modules. Let's assume we are talking about a fictitious online shop in this case. For modules that are heavily interdependent, for example, Order and Customer, it will be complex to extract them individually. If you also consider the necessity for scalability and with that the benefit of removing them from a monolith, it might not be very high. Those two modules reside on the lower left side of the graph. On the opposite side, we might find the Catalog service. It lists the available products and is a read-only service with very little interdependencies. During high demand on the website, this is the number-one requested module, and it benefits heavily from being extracted, as shown in Figure 5-1, indicated by the green module in the upper right of the graph. Do a similar exercise for all the modules in your application to assess cost versus benefit.

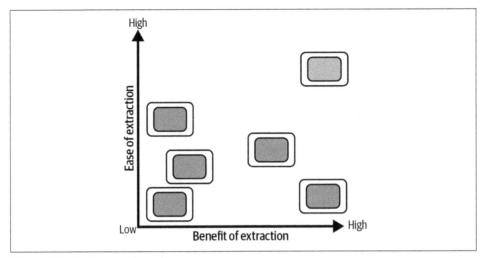

*Figure 5-1. Cost versus benefit*

You've now reached the last checkpoint to validate your earlier strategic application assessment. Does the estimated modernization benefit outweigh the estimated modernization cost? Unfortunately, there is no generally applicable recommendation, as it heavily depends on the application itself, the business requirements, and the overarching company goals and challenges. Document your decisions and conclusions because now is the time to decide about the future direction of your modernization effort. Remember the 6 Rs from Chapter 3? Retain (change nothing), Retire (turn off), Repurchase (a new version), Rehost (put into containers), Replatform (some slight adjustments), or Refactor (build something new).

We've now assessed the application for migration, and we've evaluated the functionality for migration. We know which aspects of the application we're ready to modernize. You've concluded that you do not want to build a new application but rather gently modernize the existing legacy. In the next section, we are going to take a deeper look at some approaches to migration.

# Migration Approaches

The aforementioned tools and assessments will help you on your journey to identify the most suitable applications and services. Now it's time to dig deeper into the strategies and challenges of a single application.

## Protecting Legacy (Replatform)

With only one or two modules needing a business refresh or added functionality, the most straightforward way is to focus on the two modules and keep as much as possible of the existing application, making it runnable on modern infrastructure. Besides changes of the relevant modules, this also involves a reevaluation of the runtime, libraries, or even target infrastructure while touching as little code as possible.

This can be achieved by simply containerizing the application and databases and modifying relevant modules of a well-architected monolith or extracting certain functionality completely and reintegrating it to a partly distributed system, as Figure 5-2 shows.

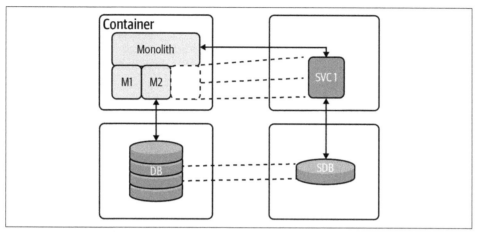

*Figure 5-2. Putting the pieces back together*

What is easily said isn't quickly done. There are plenty of nonfunctional requirements that need to be reallocated from the application server platform to the outer architecture (*https://oreil.ly/rrcZG*). We will focus on the more critical pieces in the next chapter. In this chapter, we want to focus on the migration of the application and database itself.

### Service to application

Once you've extracted certain functionality, the most pressing question is how to integrate the remaining monolith with the newly extracted service. Assuming that you switch to a container runtime, you should use an API Gateway to load balance and switch traffic on a URL basis. We'll cover this in more detail in Chapter 6.

Another approach is to use an HTTP proxy. It is essential to have the proxy up in production before you even try to extract parts of the monolith. Ensure it does not break the existing monolith and take some time to push the new service into production regularly, even without it being used by end users. Gradually switch over by redirecting traffic if everything looks good.

For more simple service to monolith interactions, you can even think about implementing a simple JAX-RS direct communication. This approach is only suitable when you work with very few services, though. Make sure to treat the extracted service as an integration system from the perspective of the monolith.

All three approaches (API, gateway, HTTP proxy, and JAX-RS interface) are a pathway to your first successful microservice. They all implement the strangler pattern (refer to Chapter 3) and help to refactor the monolith into separate systems as a first step.

Interception is a potentially dangerous path: if you start building a custom protocol translation layer that is shared by multiple services, you risk adding too much intelligence to the shared proxy. This design approach leads away from independent microservices and becomes a more service-oriented architecture with too much intelligence in the routing layer. A better alternative is the so-called Sidecar pattern, which basically describes an additional container in the Pod. Rather than placing custom proxy logic in a shared layer, it becomes part of the new service. As a Kubernetes sidecar, it becomes a runtime binding and can serve legacy clients and new clients.

A *sidecar* is just a container that runs on the same Pod as the application container. It shares the same volume and network as the application container and can "help" or enhance application behavior with this. Typical examples are logging, or more generally agent functionality.

### Database to databases

Once we have identified the functional boundary and the integration method, we need to decide how to approach database separation. While monolith applications typically rely on a single large database, each extracted service should operate on its own data. The correct way to solve this puzzle again depends on the existing data layout and transactions.

A relatively easy first step is to separate the tables necessary for the service into a read-only view and a write table and adjust the flow of the monolith to use an interface for both read and write operations. These interfaces can more easily be abstracted in a later step into a service access. This option requires changes to the monolith application only and should have minimal impact on the existing codebase. We can move the table into a separate database and adjust the dependent queries in the next step.

All this solely happens in the old monolith as preparation. Evolving existing code into a more modularized structure as preparation can be risky. In particular, the risk increases as the data model complexity does. In the last step, we can separate the extracted tables into a new database and adjust the monolith to use the newly created service for interactions with the business object. This is relatively easy with pen and paper and quickly reaches the end of practicality if the data access requires many joins across tables. Simple candidates are master data objects, like "User." More complex ones could be combined objects, like an "Order." What was said about the modularization of the application code is even more true for the database. The better the design and modularization already are, the easier it will be to extract functionality and data into a separate service. There will be cases where you won't find an excellent solution to extract objects from the data model. Or you may see different approaches not delivering suitable performance anymore. This is the time to revisit your chosen modernization path.

Continuing on the happy path, you now have two separate databases and two very unequal "services" composing a system. Now it's time to think about data synchronization strategies between your services. Most databases implement some functionality to execute behavior on data changes. Simple cases support trigger functionality on changed rows to add copies to other tables or even call higher-level features (e.g., WebServices) on change. It is often proprietary functionality and heavily depends on the database being used. This could be an option if you have a company-wide directive to use certain features or you're confident enough in further altering the original legacy database.

If this isn't possible, there's the batch job-based synchronization. Changed timestamps, versions, or status columns indicate a needed replication. You can rely on this as a very mature and well-known version of data synchronization, which you can find in many legacy systems. The major drawback is that you'll always end up with a discrepancy in data accuracy in the target system no matter the implementation. Higher replication intervals might also lead to additional costs for transactions or additional load on the source system. This approach is only suitable for infrequent updates that ideally have a non-time-sensitive process step in between. It is unsuitable for real- or near-time update requirements.

The modern approach to solving data synchronization challenges relies on log readers. As third-party libraries, they identify changes by scanning the database transaction log files. These log files exist for backup and recovery operations and provide a reliable way to capture all changes, including deletes. This concept is also known as change-data-capture. One of the most notable projects here is Debezium (*https:// debezium.io*). Using log readers is the least disruptive option for synchronizing changes between databases because they require no modification to the source database, and they don't have a query load on the source systems. Change data events generate notifications for other systems with the help of the Outbox pattern.

## Build Something New (Refactor)

If, for whatever reasons, you've reached a fork in the road where you decide to re-implement and refactor your complete system into a new distributed architecture, you are most likely thinking about synergies and ways to keep effort small and predictable. Given the complexity of a full microservices stack, this isn't an easy task. One critical factor with this approach is team knowledge. After many years of development on an Enterprise Java application server, a team should profit from continuous API and standards knowledge. There are various ways to implement services on the JVM that all help teams with reusing the most critical functionalities we all already know from Enterprise Java/Jakarta EE standards. Let's discuss some of these methods for implementing services on the JVM.

 Jakarta EE (*https://jakarta.ee/about*) is a set of specifications that enables Java developers to work on Java Enterprise applications. The specifications are developed by well-known industry leaders that instill confidence in technology developers and consumers. It is the open source version of the Java Enterprise Edition.

## MicroProfile

MicroProfile (*https://microprofile.io*) was created in 2016 and quickly joined the Eclipse foundation. The primary purpose of MicroProfile is to create a Java Enterprise framework for implementing portable microservices in a vendor-neutral way. MicroProfile is composed of a vendor-agnostic programming model and configuration and services such as tracing, fault tolerance, health, and metrics. MicroProfile API components are built upon the model of Jakarta EE, making a transition to microservices more natural for Java developers. You can reuse the existing knowledge of Jakarta EE you've already accumulated in your career. MicroProfile defines 12 specifications as shown in Figure 5-3, and the component model underneath uses a subset of the existing Jakarta EE standards. Compared to the full Jakarta EE specification, the more heavyweight specifications are missing. Most relevant for larger monolithic applications are Enterprise JavaBeans (EJB) and Jakarta XML Web Services.

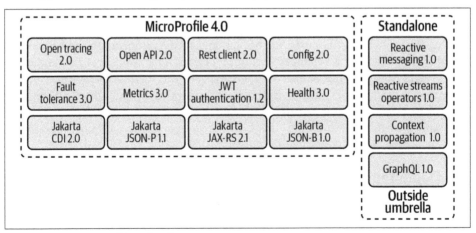

*Figure 5-3. MicroProfile technologies overview*

There are various implementations of the MicroProfile specifications available: Open Liberty, Thorntail, Paraya Server, TomEE, SmallRye, etc. As the MicroProfile relies on principles and components close to the Jakarta EE Web Profile, it is comparably easy to migrate existing applications.

## Quarkus

Quarkus (*http://quarkus.io*) is a relatively new member of the so-called microservices frameworks. It is a full stack, Kubernetes-native Java framework for JVMs and native compilation. It is optimized specifically for containers and constrained runtime environments. Its primary purpose is to be an ideal runtime for serverless, cloud, and Kubernetes environments.

It works with popular Java standards, frameworks, and libraries like Eclipse Micro-Profile, Spring Boot, Apache Kafka, RESTEasy (JAX-RS), Hibernate ORM (JPA), Infinispan, Camel, and many more.

The dependency injection solution is based on CDI (Contexts and Dependency Injection) coming from Jakarta EE, making it compatible with established component models. An interesting part is the extension framework, which helps expand functionality to configure, boot, and integrate company-specific libraries into your application. It runs on JVMs and supports GraalVM (a general-purpose virtual machine for many languages).

## Component models to services

One of the most common questions among developers is how to migrate existing component models of Enterprise Java applications into microservices. Commonly, this question refers to Enterprise Java Beans or CDI Beans, especially the container-managed persistence beans (before EJB3), which need to be re-created on a Java Persistence API (JPA) basis. We strongly recommend checking if the underlying data/object mapping is still accurate and suitable for the new requirements and re-creating it entirely. This is not the most time- and cost-consuming part of modernization. Typically, the more challenging parts are the coded business requirements. While CDI Beans are technically part of MicroProfile-compatible implementations, the decision of whether a simple code migration is appropriate depends on the new business requirements. It is essential to look for existing code transaction boundaries to ensure no downstream resource needs to be involved. A general recommendation is to reuse as little source code as possible. The reason here is mainly the different approaches in system design between the two technologies. While we got away with a halfway modularized monolith, this isn't possible with microservices anymore. Taking extra care to define the bounded contexts will pay off for the performance and design of the final solution.

### Spring applications to services

We can take a similar approach with applications following a different programming framework like Spring. While it will technically be easy to update and copy existing implementations, the drawbacks stay the same. In particular, it might be helpful for Spring-based development teams to use compatibility APIs in different frameworks like Quarkus.

Quarkus's Spring API compatibility includes Spring DI, Spring Web, and Spring Data JPA. Additional Spring APIs are partially supported like Spring Security, Spring Cache, Spring Scheduled, and Spring Cloud Config. The Spring API compatibility in Quarkus is not intended to be a complete Spring platform to rehost existing Spring applications. The intent is to offer enough Spring API compatibility to develop new applications with Quarkus.

# Challenges

With assessment, planning, and care, you can decompose and modernize existing monolithic applications. It is not an automated process most of the time and will require a decent amount of work. There are some specific challenges to watch out for.

## Avoiding Dual-Writes

Once you build a few microservices, you quickly realize that the most challenging part about them is data. As part of their business logic, microservices often have to update their local data store. At the same time, they also need to notify other services about the changes that happened. This challenge is not so evident in the world of monolithic applications, nor on legacy-distributed transactions operating on one data model. This situation isn't easy to resolve. With a switch to distributed applications, you most likely lose consistency. This is described in the CAP theorem.

 The CAP theorem (*https://oreil.ly/TVwYw*), or the "two out of three" concept, states that we can only simultaneously provide two of the following three guarantees: consistency, availability, and partitition tolerance.

Modern distributed applications use an event bus, like Apache Kafka, to transport data between services. Migrating your transactions from two-phase commit (2PC) in your monolith to a distributed world will significantly change the way your application behaves and reacts to failures. You need a way to control long-running and distributed transactions.

## Long-Running Transactions

The Saga pattern offers a solution to dual writes and long-running transactions. While the Outbox pattern solves the more straightforward interservice communication problem, it is insufficient to solve the more complex, long-running, distributed business transactions use case. The latter requires executing multiple operations across multiple services with a consistent all-or-nothing semantic. Every multistep business process can be an example of this when split out across multiple services. The shopping cart application needs to generate confirmation emails and print a shipping label in the inventory. All actions must be carried out together or not at all. In the legacy world, or with a monolithic architecture, you might not be aware of this problem as the coordination between the modules is done in a single process and a single transactional context. The distributed world requires a different approach.

The Saga pattern offers a solution to this problem by splitting up an overarching business transaction into multiple local database transactions, which are executed by the participating services. Generally, there are two ways to implement distributed sagas:

- Choreography: In this approach, one participating service sends a message to the next one after it has executed its local transaction.
- Orchestration: In this approach, one central coordinating service coordinates and invokes the participating services. Communication between the participating services might be either synchronous, via HTTP or gRPC, or asynchronous, via messaging such as Apache Kafka.

## Removing Old Code Too Quickly

As soon as we extract a service, we want to get rid of the old source code, maintenance costs, and duplicate development. But be careful. You can look at the old code as a reference and test changes in behavior against both code bases. It might also be helpful from time to time to check the timing of the newly created service. A recommendation is to run them side by side for a defined period and compare the results. After this, you can remove the old implementation. That is early enough.

# Integration Aspects

Traditional monoliths have a solid relationship with complex integration logic. This is mainly proxied behind session facades or integrated with data synchronization logic. Every single system integrated into the overarching business process needs to be treated as a separate service. You can apply the same principles when extracting parts of the data from the existing data model and do this step by step. Another approach is to treat your integration logic as a service from the very beginning. A method that was primarily designed to support microservices is Camel K (*https://oreil.ly/JiOwc*). It builds on the foundation of the well-known Apache Camel integration library and wraps integration routes into containers or better individual services. This way, you can separate the complete integration logic of your monolithic application and your services.

## Summary

Modern enterprise Java systems are like generations of families: they evolve on top of legacy systems. Using proven patterns, standardized tools, and open source resources will help you create long-lasting systems that can grow and change with your needs. Fundamentally, your migration approach is directly related to what problems you're trying to solve today and tomorrow. What are you trying to achieve that your current architecture doesn't scale up to? Maybe microservices are the answer, or perhaps something else is. You must understand what you're trying to achieve because it will be challenging to establish how to migrate the existing systems without that comprehension. Understanding your end goal will change how you decompose a system and how you prioritize that work.

# CHAPTER 6

# Building Kubernetes-Native Applications

In the previous chapter, we outlined how to migrate from the traditional Java enterprise pattern to a container-centric approach. In this chapter, we will walk through the components needed to migrate to microservices-based architectures and how Kubernetes can connect the dots.

We also learned in previous chapters how much a microservices-based approach helps to make our software reliable, portable, and ready to scale upon demand. Modern architectures are planned with scalability already in the scope since the beginning, and this offers both opportunities and challenges. Enterprise Java developers know their code is usually part of the business logic, relying on frameworks to make it robust and consistent with well-recognized software design patterns. It is more common today that the same application could serve millions of requests running on a public cloud, even distributed geographically. To do that, it has to be architected to fit this model, decoupling functions, avoiding a single point of failure, and distributing the load to several parts of the architecture to avoid service interruptions.

## Find the Right Balance Between Scalability and Complexity

In an ideal world, all applications would be stateless, and they could scale up independently. They wouldn't crash, and the network links would always be reliable. The reality looks different. The migration from monoliths to microservices-based architectures enables cloud native deployments, and we've covered some of the benefits that brings. However, that also brings some challenges: managing multiple points of ingress for your app, keeping the relationships between multiple microservices consistent, and managing distributed databases and schemas.

In Figure 6-1, you can see how the transition from monolithic to microservices-based apps brings a new approach, having multiple interconnections or even multiple databases to work with.

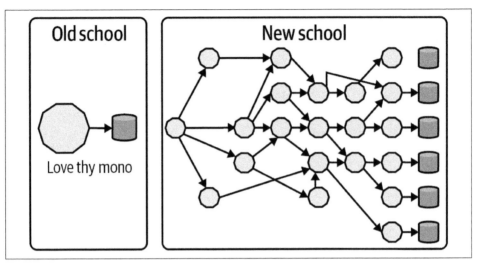

*Figure 6-1. From monolith to microservices architectures*

Similar to the CAP theorem (*https://oreil.ly/nruM5*), it is very hard to simultaneously provide scalability without increasing the complexity of a system. That's why Kubernetes is so helpful because it's ubiquitous, it runs in any cloud, and you can delegate most of this complexity to this platform. This lets you focus "just" on app development. On the other hand, we need to find a solution also for *stateful* apps in the cloud native world, and we will see that Kubernetes also provides help on this side.

## Functional Requirements for Modern Architectures

Kubernetes is very helpful with defining distributed applications as shown in Figure 3-1. Any Java developer should be well aware of Design Patterns (*https://oreil.ly/V4aqC*) from Gang of Four, a masterpiece of software engineering where authors define the most-used software design patterns. Kubernetes extends this set of patterns, creating a new set of cloud native specific requirements to make applications resilient to various loads as shown in Figure 6-2. Let's dig into some of those in the next sections.

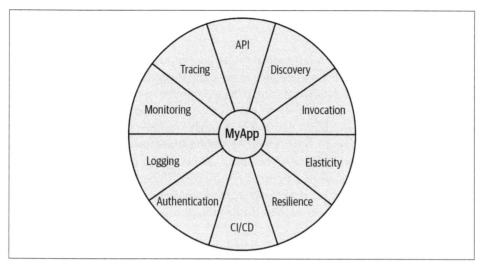

*Figure 6-2. Functional requirements for modern architectures*

## API-Driven

The microservices mantra is "API first." If you take a look again at Figure 6-1, you'll notice that splitting a monolithic app into a bunch of microservices leads to the first challenge: how to let these pieces of software communicate with each other? In monoliths, you rely on the app scope of modules, packages. Microservices usually communicate with each other via REST calls, where each one can be either producer or consumer of services. This is not the only way to connect your microservices; it's also a common use case to use queues, messages, or caches. But in general, each microservice exposes its primitives or functions through a set of APIs, and this can also be intermediated by an API gateway as we discussed in the Coolstore example in Chapter 2.

Kubernetes itself is API-driven software. All core components of the platform such as Pods, Services, and Deployments are manipulated through REST APIs. All operations and communications between components and external user commands are REST API calls that the API server handles (*https://oreil.ly/PauGF*). When we interact with Kubernetes through kubectl or JKube, we are just invoking an API via HTTPS sending and receiving JSON content. This ecosystem of APIs is the perfect environment for an API-driven architecture, such as one that uses microservices. Now that we know how our microservices communicate, how do we discover new services?

# Discovery

It's pretty straightforward to let microservices communicate with each other using REST calls. In addition, it would be nice to have the invocation of other components and functions at ease, such as when importing a module or a package into our app. In modern architectures, the number of microservices to invoke and connect could potentially be pretty high, thus it may not be enough to simply store the network endpoints such as IP address or hostnames. As we discussed in Chapter 4, Kubernetes simplifies networking with the `Service` object, allowing two or more Pods to talk to each other within the platform's internal networking. Kubernetes also provides the capability to list objects inside the cluster from an application, thanks to its API. Java developers can use frameworks such as JKube to have a Java Kubernetes client for this purpose.

Listing Kubernetes Services and Pods, which represent some microservices, is the first step to a real-time inventory of components of our software stack, which additionally helps to maintain and extend at runtime applications. Furthermore, Kubernetes enables integration with external tools or frameworks for that, such as Service Mesh, which provides service discovery protocol to detect services as they come up.

Service mesh (*https://oreil.ly/jGh80*) is an increasingly popular choice for microservices-based architectures. It provides a control panel that also interacts with Kubernetes to manage service discovery, mutual authentication, A/B testing, routing, and circuit breaker pattern out of the box. Further details can be found online (*https://oreil.ly/ECIF4*).

# Security and Authorization

Another challenge that modern app developers need to take into account is security for the entire stack. From the app to the platform, best practices also apply to modern architectures, and the complexity and the required effort may rise significantly when there are many services to connect, many databases to query, and many endpoints to serve. Again, Kubernetes comes in to help.

Kubernetes provides security for the entire ecosystem. Role-based access control (RBAC) and fine-grained permission rules are possible. Furthermore, Pods are run by a special user called *Service Account* that has access to the Kubernetes API Server, usually having limited scope to the user's namespace. Besides that, Kubernetes provides a special API to manage passwords and certificates called *Secrets*. A Secret is a volume mounted into the Pod by the platform at runtime, with its value stored into Kubernetes's database etcd, along with cluster state and configurations.

etcd (*https://etcd.io*) is a distributed key-value database used by Kubernetes to store the cluster state. The content of the database can be also encrypted, and only the cluster administrator can access its content.

As we discussed, the communication between microservices is usually done via HTTPS REST calls, whose certificates are managed via Secrets. Containers and Kubernetes provide a good starting point for ensuring security in applications, from which Java developers can start to implement app security best practices.

## Monitoring

Measuring resource consumption is essential in modern architectures, and ever more so in cloud environments with a pay-per-use consumption model. It isn't easy to estimate how many computational resources your app will need under stress, and overestimation may increase costs. Kubernetes enables monitoring at the operating system level to application level, with its ecosystem of API and tools.

A popular cloud native tool to gather metrics from the platform and the app is Prometheus (*https://prometheus.io*), a time-series database that can export metrics from the Kubernetes cluster and apps using a query language called PromQL (*https://oreil.ly/tYn9Q*).

Metrics are also used to help Kubernetes decide when to scale your application up or down according to the monitored load on the app. You can drive this scale with custom metrics, such as JVM threads or queue size, and make monitoring a proactive tool to empower your services. Prometheus also provides alerts and alarms, which are useful to schedule automated actions for your applications when they need to react faster.

Java developers can also interact with Prometheus and metrics inside Kubernetes with Micrometer (*https://micrometer.io*), an open source tool that provides a registration mechanism for metrics and core metric types. It is available for any JVM-based workloads, and it is the popular choice for both Spring Boot and Quarkus projects to interact with Prometheus and Kubernetes. "Think SLF4J, but for metrics."

## Tracing

Observability is another key aspect in modern architectures, and measuring latency between REST API calls is an important facet of managing microservices-based apps. It is crucial to ensure that the communication is always clear and the latency is minimal. When the number of microservices increases, a small delay in some part of the architecture can result in an acceptable service interruption for the user. In these situations, Kubernetes is helpful for debugging the majority of operational problems that arise when moving to a distributed architecture.

Jaeger (*https://www.jaegertracing.io*) is a popular open source tool that connects to Kubernetes to provide observability. It uses distributed tracing to follow the path of a request through different microservices. It provides a visual representation of the call flows through a dashboard, and it is often also integrated with Service mesh. Jaeger is very helpful to developers for monitoring distributed transactions, optimizing performance and latency, and performing root cause analysis.

## Logging

As we discussed, a single call in your microservices-based app, such as the Coolstore example, can invoke different services that interact with each other. It's important to monitor and observe the app, but also to store relevant pieces of information in logs. Your application's logging approach changes with modern apps. While in monoliths we usually rely on multiple log files stored in different paths on the disk, usually managed by the application server, distributed apps *stream* logs. As your app can scale up rapidly and move to different nodes or even clouds, it makes no sense to access the single instance to retrieve logs; therefore, a distributed log system is needed.

Kubernetes makes logging easy as well. By default, it provides the capability to access a Pod's logs by reading the application's standard streams such as STDOUT (Standard Output) and STDERR (Standard Error). Thus, the app should not write logs into a certain path, but send logs to standard streams.

 It is still possible to store logs in specific paths that can also be persistent in Kubernetes, but this is considered an antipattern.

Kubernetes also interacts with distributed logging systems such as Elasticsearch (*https://elastic.co*), an open source document-oriented NoSQL database based on Apache Lucene (*https://lucene.apache.org*) to store logs and events. Elasticsearch usually comes with a forwarder, such as Fluentd (*https://fluentd.org*), and a dashboard to visualize logs such as Kibana (*https://elastic.co/kibana*). Together, this creates the EFK stack (Elasticsearch, Fluentd, Kibana). With this logging stack, developers consult logs from multiple microservices in an aggregated view through the Kibana dashboard, and they are also able to make queries in a query language called Kibana Query Language (KQL).

Distributed logging is the de facto standard with cloud native apps, and Kubernetes connects and interacts with many offerings such as EFK to provide centralized logging for the whole cluster.

# CI/CD

Continuous Integration (CI) is a phase in the software development cycle where code from different team members or different features is integrated. This usually involves merging code (integration), building the application (container), and carrying out basic tests, all within an ephemeral environment.

Continuous Delivery (CD) refers to a set of practices to automate various aspects of delivery software. One of these practices is called delivery pipeline, which is an automated process to define the steps a change in code or configuration has to go through to reach upper environments and eventually production.

Together, they are often referred to as CI/CD, and it is one of the key technology enablers for DevOps methodology.

Modern services need to react fast to changes or issues. As we can monitor, trace, and log distributed architectures, we should also be able to update our microservices-based app faster. Pipelines are the best way to deploy apps in production following the phases as shown in Figure 6-3.

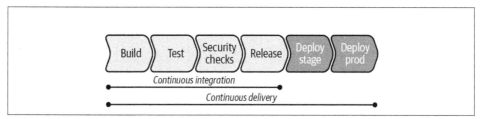

*Figure 6-3. Continuous Integration and Continuous Delivery*

A *pipeline* is a series of steps, sequential or parallel, that build and test the app in all preproduction environments before finally releasing it to production. It can be fully automated or can interact with external tools for manual step approval (e.g., Service Now, JIRA, etc.). Kubernetes interacts and connects with many external CI/CD tools such as Jenkins (*https://jenkins.io*), and also provides a native CI/CD subsystem called Tekton (*https://tekton.dev*).

Tekton is a Kubernetes-native CI/CD system, which means it extends the Kubernetes API and provides its custom resources that you can use to create your pipelines. It relies on a catalog of Tasks (*https://oreil.ly/Oxx5P*) that comes already bundled with Tekton to compose your pipelines, such as Maven or Java Source-to-Image Tasks.

 Tekton can be installed in Kubernetes with an Operator from OperatorHub.io (*https://operatorhub.io*).

To create Kubernetes-native pipelines, the following custom resources are provided by Tekton:

*Task*
> A reusable, loosely coupled number of steps that perform a specific function (e.g., building a container image). Tasks get executed as Kubernetes Pods while steps in a Task map onto containers.

*Pipeline*
> A list of Tasks needed to build and/or deploy your apps.

*TaskRun*
> The execution and result of running an instance of Task.

*PipelineRun*
> The execution and result of running an instance of Pipeline, which includes a number of TaskRuns.

An example of a Tekton Pipeline for the Inventory Quarkus microservice that we created in Chapter 2 is listed next, you can also find it in this book's GitHub repository (*https://oreil.ly/2UUCL*):

```
apiVersion: tekton.dev/v1alpha1
kind: Pipeline
metadata:
  name: inventory-pipeline
spec:
  resources:
  - name: app-git
    type: git
  - name: app-image
    type: image
  tasks:
  - name: build
    taskRef:
      name: s2i-java-11
    params:
      - name: TLSVERIFY
```

```
        value: "false"
    resources:
      inputs:
      - name: source
        resource: app-git
      outputs:
      - name: image
        resource: app-image
  - name: deploy
    taskRef:
      name: kubectl
    runAfter:
      - build
    params:
    - name: ARGS
      value:
        - rollout
        - latest
        - inventory-pipeline
```

Java developers may also find it convenient to create and control Tekton Pipelines and Tasks direcly from the code, using Fabric8 Tekton Java client. This option gives the full control from a single point, and you don't need to maintain external manifests such as YAML files.

First, import Maven dependency in POM file:

```
<dependencies>
    <dependency>
        <groupId>io.fabric8</groupId>
        <artifactId>tekton-client</artifactId>
        <version>${tekton-client.version}</version>
    </dependency>
</dependencies>
<properties>
    <tekton-client.version>4.12.0</tekton-client.version>
</properties>
```

Then you can use Tekton Java API to create Tasks or Pipeline:

```
package io.fabric8.tekton.api.examples;

import io.fabric8.tekton.client.*;
import io.fabric8.tekton.resource.v1alpha1.PipelineResource;
import io.fabric8.tekton.resource.v1alpha1.PipelineResourceBuilder;

public class PipelineResourceCreate {

  public static void main(String[] args) {
    try ( TektonClient client = ClientFactory.newClient(args)) {
      String namespace = "coolstore";
      PipelineResource resource = new PipelineResourceBuilder()
        .withNewMetadata()
```

```
        .withName("client-repo")
        .endMetadata()
        .withNewSpec()
        .withType("git")
        .addNewParam()
        .withName("revision")
        .withValue("v4.2.2")
        .endParam()
        .addNewParam()
        .withName("url")
        .withValue("https://github.com/modernizing-java-applications-book/
          inventory-quarkus.git")
        .endParam()
        .endSpec()
        .build();

    System.out.println("Created:" + client.v1alpha1().pipelineResources().
      inNamespace(namespace).create(resource).getMetadata().getName());
    }
  }
}
```

## Debugging Microservices

While distributed architectures have plenty of benefits, they also pose some chal‐
lenges. Even if you eventually run your code inside a Kubernetes cluster, you still
develop (in general) locally where you have your IDE, compilers, etc. There are sev‐
eral ways to explain the development cycle. There are two loops, as illustrated in
Figure 6-4. The one closer to the developer, called the inner loop, is where you code,
test, and debug iteratively. The other loop, further away from the developer, called the
outer loop, is where your code runs inside a container image you have to build, push,
and deploy, and that takes a lot longer.

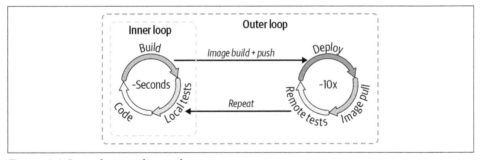

*Figure 6-4. Inner loop and outer loop*

While the outer loop is part of the CI/CD world, the inner loop is where you start
coding and testing your software before launching a Tekton Pipeline to deploy your
application into Kubernetes. Debugging microservices is also part of the inner loop.

Developers can follow different approaches to start debugging microservices:

- Using Docker Compose (*https://oreil.ly/ULV5g*) and deploying all the services locally
- Using minikube (*https://oreil.ly/1ogSc*), or any local Kubernetes clusters, and deploying all the services there
- Mocking up all the services you interact with

 Docker Compose helps create containers that run in any Docker hosts, without Kubernetes. It is used for managing multiple containers in local development, but it is not mapped to any target Kubernetes clusters; thus, maintaining the local development setup separate from the target one may be difficult.

They are all valid approaches, but there are times where services are external and reachable only from the remote Kubernetes cluster, or mocking up that part of code is difficult or not possible.

Microcks (*https://microcks.io*) is an open source Kubernetes-native debugging tool for API mocking and testing. It helps turn API contract, collection, or SoapUI projects into live mocks. It can be a convenient way to develop faster on Kubernetes without dependencies.

Let's look at some additional options for in-Kubernetes microservices debugging.

## Port Forwarding

Kubernetes offers remote shelling into Pods for quick debugging tasks such as filesystem check. Additionally, you can set up port forwarding (*https://oreil.ly/IAu5H*) between your local machine connected to a Kubernetes cluster and your app running in a Pod. This option is useful when you want to connect to a database running in a Pod, attach an administrative web interface you don't want to expose to the public, or, in this case, attach a debugger to the JVM running our application server.

By port forwarding the debugging port for the application server, you can attach the debugger from your IDE and actually step through the code in the Pod as it is running in real time. Remember, if your app is not in debug mode, you first need to turn on the debug ports.

To start debugging, you need to expose the port for debugging. For example, for debugging the Inventory microservice, you need to access the debugging port 5005:

```
kubectl port-forward service/inventory-quarkus 5005:5005
```

Now when we connect on *localhost:5005*, it will get forwarded to the Inventory instance running in the Pod.

 Port forwarding is only active as long as the `kubectl port-forward` command is allowed to run. Since we run it in the foreground, we are able to stop port forwarding by hitting Ctrl+C (or Cmd+C on a Mac).

In order to debug the source code, you can either use your IDE of choice or you can debug from the console as follows:

```
jdb -sourcepath $(pwd)/src/main/java -attach localhost:5005
```

## Quarkus Remote Development Mode

Quarkus provides a Remote Development Mode (*https://oreil.ly/rLflo*) that allows you to run Quarkus in a container environment such as Kubernetes and have changes made to your local files immediately.

To enable it, add this section in your `application.properties`:

```
quarkus.package.type=mutable-jar ❶
quarkus.live-reload.password=changeit ❷
quarkus.live-reload.url=http://my.cluster.host.com:8080 ❸
```

❶ Mutable applications are used in development mode to apply and test changes live in a Quarkus Java application, without reloading the artifact.

❷ A password that is used to secure communication between the remote side and the local side.

❸ The URL at which your app is going to be running in dev mode.

You can generate the mutable JAR with Maven. You can let Quarkus deploy the app to Kubernetes as follows if you are connected with the Kubernetes Registry:

```
eval $(minikube docker-env)
```

 You can add the Quarkus Kubernetes extension with this command: `./mvnw quarkus:add-extension -Dextensions="kubernetes"`

Deploy the app to Kubernetes:

```
mvn clean install -DskipTests -Dquarkus.kubernetes.deploy=true
```

Finally, you connect in remote dev mode to the app:

```
mvn quarkus:remote-dev
```

This allows you to use Quarkus to connect the live coding features from your local machine to a remote container environment such as Kubernetes.

## Telepresence

Telepresence (*https://www.telepresence.io*) is an open source tool that helps debug microservices in Kubernetes. It runs a single service locally, while connecting that service to a remote Kubernetes cluster. Telepresence is programming language-agnostic, providing a convenient way to connect your local enviroment to any workload running on Kubernetes to debug.

Debugging apps on Kubernetes with Telepresence is very easy. First, download and install Telepresence CLI (*https://oreil.ly/wkwOC*) and have an active session to your cluster, as Telepresence will read the *~/.kube/config* file to connect to Kubernetes.

 Telepresence will modify the network in Kubernetes so that Services are reachable from your laptop and vice versa.

Once the CLI is installed and configured in your workstation, you can run this command to initialize and test the connection to your cluster with Telepresence:

```
$ telepresence connect
```

You should get an output similar to the following:

```
Connected to context minikube (https://192.168.39.69:8443)
```

We can start debugging the Inventory microservice that you deployed in the previous steps. Before doing that, let's list available apps to debug:

```
$ telepresence list
```

You should get an output similar to the following:

```
inventory-quarkus-deploy: ready to intercept (traffic-agent not yet installed)
```

To start debugging this microservice, you need to let Telepresence intercept the internal Kubernetes traffic represented by the Service.

The Inventory's Kubernetes Service is using port 8080, as you can see with the following command:

```
$ kubectl get svc inventory-quarkus-service
```

You should get an output similar to the following:

```
NAME                       TYPE       CLUSTER-IP      EXTERNAL-IP PORT(S)  AGE
inventory-quarkus-service ClusterIP 172.30.117.178 <none>       8080/TCP 84m
```

Now you can start intercepting the traffic connecting to your Deployment with the port used by the Service. You can also specify the path to a file on which Telepresence should write the environment variables that your service is currently running with:

```
$ telepresence intercept inventory-quarkus-deploy --port 8080:http --env-file
    inventory.env
```

You should get an output similar to the following:

```
Using Deployment inventory-quarkus-deploy
intercepted
    Intercept name         : inventory-quarkus-deploy
    State                  : ACTIVE
    Workload kind          : Deployment
    Destination            : 127.0.0.1:8080
    Service Port Identifier: http
    Volume Mount Point     : /tmp/telfs-844792531
    Intercepting           : all TCP connections
```

Look at the content of the environment file inventory.env just created:

```
INVENTORY_QUARKUS_SERVICE_PORT=tcp://172.30.117.178:8080
INVENTORY_QUARKUS_SERVICE_PORT_8080_TCP=tcp://172.30.117.178:8080
INVENTORY_QUARKUS_SERVICE_PORT_8080_TCP_ADDR=172.30.117.178
INVENTORY_QUARKUS_SERVICE_PORT_8080_TCP_PORT=8080
INVENTORY_QUARKUS_SERVICE_PORT_8080_TCP_PROTO=tcp
INVENTORY_QUARKUS_SERVICE_SERVICE_HOST=172.30.117.178
INVENTORY_QUARKUS_SERVICE_SERVICE_PORT=8080
INVENTORY_QUARKUS_SERVICE_SERVICE_PORT_HTTP=8080
KO_DATA_PATH=/var/run/ko
KUBERNETES_PORT=tcp://172.30.0.1:443
KUBERNETES_PORT_443_TCP=tcp://172.30.0.1:443
KUBERNETES_PORT_443_TCP_ADDR=172.30.0.1
KUBERNETES_PORT_443_TCP_PORT=443
KUBERNETES_PORT_443_TCP_PROTO=tcp
KUBERNETES_SERVICE_HOST=172.30.0.1
KUBERNETES_SERVICE_PORT=443
KUBERNETES_SERVICE_PORT_HTTPS=443
LOG_LEVEL=debug
NSS_SDB_USE_CACHE=no
TELEPRESENCE_CONTAINER=inventory-quarkus
TELEPRESENCE_MOUNTS=/var/run/secrets/kubernetes.io
TELEPRESENCE_ROOT=/tmp/telfs-777636888
TERM=xterm
```

Now you can access the Inventory microservice as if you were connected to the internal Kubernetes network, and working with the environment variables just retrieved:

```
curl http://inventory-quarkus-service.coolstore:8080/api/inventory/329299
```

You should get an output similar to the following:

```
{"id":"329299","quantity":35}
```

# Summary

In this chapter, we discussed how Kubernetes patterns can help Java developers with modernizing their apps, offering a platform that provides many components to extend app capabilities. The API-driven, pluggable architecture of Kubernetes easily enables external tools to provide an ecosystem of software and utilities that reminds, but also extends the application server model for Java enterprise. Essential tasks such as logging, monitoring, or debugging apps are provided in a way that fits the cloud native model, where apps are ubiquituous and can run in multiple places and multiple clouds at the same time.

In the next chapter, we will discuss a new concept of serving and delivering the enterprise application, resource-saving and cloud-ready: the serverless way.

# CHAPTER 7

# Tomorrow's Solutions: Serverless

The second industrial revolution, unlike the first, does not present us with such crushing images as rolling mills and molten steel, but with "bits" in a flow of information traveling along with circuits in the form of electronic impulses. The iron machines still exist, but they obey the orders of weightless bits.

—Italo Calvino

The serverless computing model has great momentum with public cloud offerings, and recently also within the open source community thanks to many projects that enable it for any platform. But, what is serverless, exactly? What are some use cases for serverless? And, how can it be used for modern Java applications?

## What Is Serverless?

The best definition of serverless comes from the CNCF Serverless Whitepaper (*https://oreil.ly/yYbmP*):

> Serverless computing refers to the concept of building and running applications that do not require server management. It describes a finer-grained deployment model where applications, bundled as one or more functions, are uploaded to a platform and then executed, scaled, and billed in response to the exact demand needed at the moment.

Running an application that "does not require server management" is the most relevant part of that definition. In the previous chapters, we explored how Kubernetes helps with functional requirements for modern architectures, and how container images represent a convenient way to package and ship applications to any cloud platform. There are still servers in serverless, however, they are abstracted away from app development. While a third party handles the complexity of maintaining and managing such servers, developers can simply package their code in containers for deployment.

The main differentiator between the deployment model that we discussed in Kubernetes and the serverless model is the so-called *scale-to-zero* approach. With this approach, an application is automatically launched on demand when called, and idle when not used. This execution model is also called event-driven, and it is the core foundation of serverless. We discuss event-driven serverless architectures later in this chapter.

Typically, a series of events can trigger the launch of the application, which will produce an outcome, as you can see in Figure 7-1. This can be a single action or a chain of actions where the output of one app is the input of the subsequent app. The event can be anything, such as an HTTP request, a Kafka message, or a database transaction. The application can be autoscaled to multiple replicas proportional to the needed amount to handle the traffic load, and then scaled down when there isn't any activity.

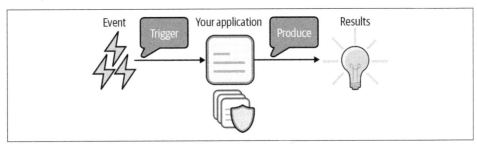

*Figure 7-1. Serverless execution model*

## Architectural Evolution

The serverless model is not good for all use cases. In general, any asynchronous, concurrent, easy-to-parallelize-into-independent-units-of-work application is a good fit for this model. If you look at the diagram in Figure 7-2, you can see how the microservices-based architectures evolution started from a monolithic applications approach using the service-oriented architectures (SOA) model, and it is now evolving again into a new model of *functions*.

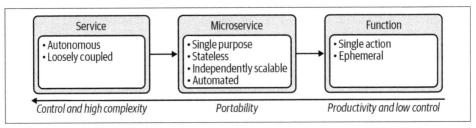

*Figure 7-2. Architectural evolution*

These functions represent a minimal computing unit that accomplishes a specific scope or task. Examples are:

- Processing web hooks
- Data transformation (image, video)
- PDF generation
- Single-page apps for mobile devices
- Chatbots

With this approach, you can focus on convenience, as it is generally offered as *best-effort*. Failures are tolerated, and short actions are preferred. That's why the serverless model is not good for use cases such as real-time applications, long-running tasks, or contexts where reliability and/or atomicity are key. It's up to the developer to take care of verifying that inputs and outputs have been successfully processed by any serverless function involved. This gives great flexibility and high scalability to at least some part of the overall architecture.

# Use Cases: Data, AI, and Machine Learning

The serverless model helps avoid common headaches for capacity planning for projects, as it mitigates overprovisioning and underprovisioning, thereby reducing the IT cost of idle resources. With serverless, all of the resources consumed are tailored to the actual usage as the applications start only when invoked, and there's no need to preallocate or measure-and-update hardware resources.

This is very important when you have to analyze in real time a large amount of data, and that's why serverless is gaining lots of attention from data scientists and ML experts, as the functions that can process data for analysis are flexible and leave a minimal footprint. On the other hand, serverless doesn't pair well with all of the design principles of existing ML frameworks. A certain amount of tolerance is also required, in particular for processes that may take longer such as model training.

If you look at Figure 7-3, you will see an example of a serverless-driven architecture for machine learning for classification and prediction. The process starts with a trigger to get an inference of a group of objects from a trained model. This starts a sequence of asynchronous functions that run in parallel, used to predict the class of the object based on its characteristics and return the classification as output. The tolerance we expect is that one of these functions may fail or not complete the task in time. However, those are all independent workloads. It's important to have workloads that can run in parallel without a specific order so any failure to a single function is not affecting the whole system. In addition, the autoscaling component of the serverless architecture will make sure that any high data load will be processed faster on demand than with traditional approaches.

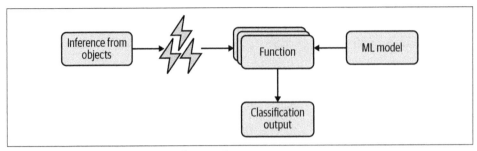

*Figure 7-3. Machine Learning with serverless*

# Use Cases: Edge Computing and IoT

Edge and IoT devices are everywhere. From vocal assistants to home automation, nowadays nearly every item in our house can be connected to the internet, talking to some controller application. As a developer, you may be responsible for either the backend logic or the device application logic.

An example of this scenario for Java developers comes from the Quarkus for IoT (*https://oreil.ly/0Lmiu*) project, which aims to collect pollution data from sensors with Raspberry Pi devices (*https://raspberrypi.org*) using Quarkus and containers both on the device and the server-side backend. The latter is running a serverless application to provide on-demand high scalability of the huge amount of sensor data that may come in some bursty way.

The project also offers a very good reference on how IoT architectures should be implemented on top of Red Hat OpenShift, as shown in Figure 7-4.

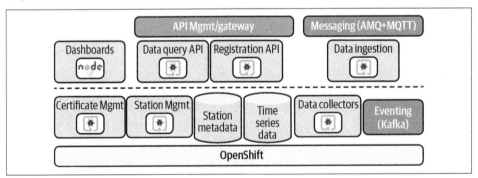

*Figure 7-4. Quarkus for IoT project architecture*

Serverless is used to scale up Quarkus microservices from device messages using the MQTT protocol for data ingestion, with Kafka streams used in the architecture as well as for data collectors. This makes the architecture complete and reliable, but also cost-efficient as there's no allocation of resources until they are needed.

# Knative: Serverless for Kubernetes

Serverless can be considered the engine of functions as a service (FaaS), which is a more convenient way for developers to package and deploy apps. Often, particularly with public clouds, serverless and FaaS fit together, since packaging apps in containers is also automated. However, a scale-to-zero app is not necessarily a function. As we discussed, serverless is not just a prerogative of public clouds. For instance, anyone can also adopt this model on any Kubernetes cluster thanks to an open source project called Knative (*https://knative.dev*).

We will discuss FaaS in more detail later in this chapter.

Knative enables serverless on Kubernetes, supporting event-driven scale-to-zero applications. It provides a higher level of abstraction for common app use cases.

Knative can easily be installed on Kubernetes through an Operator from OperatorHub.io (*https://oreil.ly/ni1wkr*).

There are two main components in Knative:

*Knative Serving*
    Takes care of scale-to-zero, creating all Kubernetes resources needed (e.g., Pod, Deployment, Service, Ingress)

*Knative Eventing*
    A subscription, delivery, and management component for handling events on-cluster and off-cluster (e.g., Kafka messages, external services)

It's easy to make an app serverless in Kubernetes with Knative. An example of a Knative Service for the Inventory Quarkus microservice that you created in Chapter 2 follows.

You can also find the example in this book's GitHub repository (*https://oreil.ly/ kyQfu*):

```
apiVersion: serving.knative.dev/v1
kind: Service ❶
metadata:
 name: inventory-svc
spec:
 template:
   spec:
     containers:
       - image: docker.io/modernizingjavaappsbook/inventory-quarkus:latest ❷
         ports:
           - containerPort: 8080
```

❶   This is the definition of Knative Service, a Custom Resource representing a serverless workload on Kubernetes.

❷   It is using the same container image we used for the Deployment object. With Knative Service, a Deployment and a Service are automatically created for you.

To create a serverless version for the Inventory microservice, you can create a Knative Service object with the following command:

```
kubectl create -f kubernetes/ksvc.yaml
```

 Knative also provides a convenient CLI called kn to create Knative Services and manage all Knative serverless components. You can find more info about it in the official documentation (*https:// oreil.ly/vDtU2*).

Immediately, you can verify that a new Knative Service has been created with this command:

```
kubectl get ksvc
```

You should get output similar to the following:

```
NAME            URL                                               ↳
LATESTCREATED       LATESTREADY          READY  REASON
inventory-svc  http://inventory-svc.coolstore.192.168.39.69.nip.io↳
   inventory-svc-00001  inventory-svc-00001  True
```

As you can see, all of the Kubernetes manifests, such as Pod, Deployment, and Service, have been created automatically from the Knative Service. There's no need to maintain them in this case, since you can rely on a single object that controls deployment and networking:

```
kubectl get deploy,pod,svc
```

```
NAME                                                 READY  UP-TO-DATE  AVAILABLE  AGE
deployment.apps/inventory-svc-00001-deployment       1/1    1           1          58m

NAME                                          READY  STATUS   RESTARTS  AGE
pod/inventory-svc-00001-deployment-58...8-8lh9b 2/2  Running  0         13s

NAME                                TYPE          CLUSTER-IP      EXTERNAL-IP
service/inventory-svc               ExternalName  <none>         ↳
kourier-internal.kourier-system.svc.cluster.local  80/TCP       58m
service/inventory-svc-00001         ClusterIP     10.109.47.140  <none>
service/inventory-svc-00001-private ClusterIP     10.101.59.10   <none>
```

Under the hood, the traffic to a Knative Service is routed into the cluster through the Knative networking. Invoking the Inventory microservice will also trigger the Pod creation if the application is idling:

```
curl http://inventory-svc.coolstore.192.168.39.69.nip.io/api/inventory/329299
```

You should get output similar to the following:

```
{"id":"329299","quantity":35}
```

After a certain amount of time with no new requests, the scale-to-zero model applies and the Pod number is scaled down to zero:

```
kubectl get deploy
NAME                              READY  UP-TO-DATE  AVAILABLE  AGE
inventory-svc-00001-deployment    0/0    0           0          75m
```

# Event-Driven Serverless Architectures

Events are everywhere. As we discussed in the previous section, an HTTP request can trigger the start of an application that can be idling when not used, which is consistent with the serverless execution model represented in Figure 7-1. But there are plenty of events out there, such as a Kafka message, a database stream, or any event from Kubernetes, that an application may want to subscribe to.

A popular pattern in this scenario is the publish-subscribe messaging pattern (*https://oreil.ly/ThcHL*) where many senders can send messages to an entity on the server, often called a topic, and receivers can subscribe to said topic to get messages. According to the serverless model, your application can be registered and connected to process incoming events. One example for Kubernetes is the Knative Eventing (*https://oreil.ly/NF2gB*) component, which implements CloudEvents (*https://cloudevents.io*), a specification for describing event data from multiple protocols and formats (such as Kafka, AMQP, and MQTT) in a common way (*https://oreil.ly/oGI1q*).

With Knative Eventing, event producers and event consumers are independent. A Knative Service is triggered by a source of events through a broker, as you can see in Figure 7-5. The goal of the eventing framework is to decouple everything. The sender doesn't directly call the subscriber or even know how many subscribers there are. Instead, brokers and triggers handle the communication.

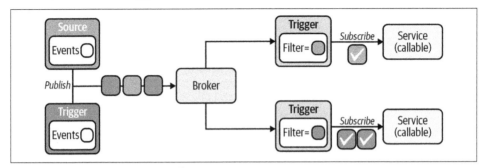

*Figure 7-5. Knative Eventing architecture*

Rather than relying on the inbound request cascading through all the microservices, you could use an arbitrary HTTP event as an example of an event to wake up the Inventory service.

First, we need to create a Knative Broker. An example of a Knative Broker for the Inventory Quarkus microservice that we created in Chapter 2 is listed below, which you can also find in this book's GitHub repository (*https://oreil.ly/8Gwys*):

```
apiVersion: eventing.knative.dev/v1
kind: Broker
metadata:
 name: default
 namespace: coolstore
```

Create the Broker:

```
kubectl create -f kubernetes/kbroker.yaml
```

You should get output similar to the following:

```
NAME     URL   AGE  READY  REASON
default  http://broker-ingress.knative-eventing...coolstore/default ↳
  11s  True
```

 We are using the internal Kubernetes networking for this part, so any endpoint we are using is a Kubernetes Service in the fully qualified domain name (FQDN) format accessible only within the cluster.

Now let's create a Trigger to wake up the Inventory microservice. It can be any event compliant with the CloudEvents specification. In this case, you can use an HTTP request from another Pod.

An example of a Knative Trigger for the Inventory Quarkus microservice that you created in Chapter 2 follows; you can find it in this book's GitHub repository (*https://oreil.ly/GmG6r*):

```
apiVersion: eventing.knative.dev/v1
kind: Trigger
metadata:
  name: inventory-trigger
spec:
  broker: default ❶
  filter:
    attributes:
      type: web-wakeup ❷
  subscriber:
    ref:
      apiVersion: serving.knative.dev/v1 ❸
      kind: Service
      name: inventory
```

❶ Name of the Broker.

❷ Attribute type. This can be used to filter which event to wake up.

❸ Name of the Knative Service to connect to and wake up to field the event.

Let's create the Knative Trigger as follows:

```
kubectl create -f kubernetes/ktrigger.yaml
```

You should get output similar to the following:

```
NAME                BROKER   SUBSCRIBER_URI  AGE  READY  REASON
inventory-trigger   default  http://inventory.coolstore...local/  10s  True
```

Now you can simulate an external event that can wake up your microservice. In this case, it's a simple HTTP call, but it can also be something like a database stream with Debezium or a Kafka message.

 Debezium.io (*https://debezium.io*) is an open source data capture platform that enables streaming from popular databases such as PostgreSQL, MySQL, etc. Check out the online documentation (*https://oreil.ly/bFEJi*) to learn more.

Run this command to download a minimal container image containing the `curl` command to run directly on Kubernetes as a Pod, sending an HTTP `POST` to the Knative Broker to trigger the microservice start:

```
kubectl run curl --image=radial/busyboxplus:curl -ti --↳
curl -v "http://broker-ingress.knative-eventing.svc.cluster.local/
  coolstore/default"
```

```
-X POST \
-H "Ce-Id: wakeup" \
-H "Ce-Specversion: 1.0" \
-H "Ce-Type: web-wakeup" \ ❶
-H "Ce-Source: web-coolstore" \ ❷
-H "Content-Type: application/json"
-d ""
```

❶  The attribute we defined in the Knative Broker before.

❷  A name for the event.

You should get output similar to the following:

```
> POST /coolstore/default HTTP/1.1
> User-Agent: curl/7.35.0
> Host: broker-ingress.knative-eventing.svc.cluster.local
> Accept: */*
> Ce-Id: wakeup
> Ce-Specversion: 1.0
> Ce-Type: web-wakeup
> Ce-Source: web-coolstore
> Content-Type: application/json
>
< HTTP/1.1 202 Accepted
< Date: Wed, 16 Jun 2021 11:03:31 GMT
< Content-Length: 0
<
```

You should now see the Inventory Pod has been started:

```
NAME                                              READY  STATUS   RESTARTS  AGE
curl                                              1/1    Running  1         30m
inventory-svc-00001-deployment-58485ffb58-kpgdt  1/2    Running  0         7s
```

# Function as a Service for Java Applications

We previously discussed how Knative Serving helps to reduce the complexity of maintaining multiple Kubernetes objects, and how scale-to-zero helps optimize resource usage by scaling down and scaling up applications on demand when needed. But there is another layer of abstraction that helps with automatically building and deploying the application following the serverless model: the FaaS model, which we introduced earlier.

FaaS is an event-driven computing execution model where developers write apps that are automatically deployed in containers fully managed by a platform, then executed on demand following the scale-to-zero model. As a developer, you don't have to write anything like a Kubernetes manifest with this model. You can simply write the application logic and let the platform package the application as a container and deploy it on the cluster as a scale-to-zero serverless app.

Popular public cloud serverless solutions such as AWS Lambda, Azure Functions, or Google Cloud Run provide a convenient SDK to start developing functions written in the most popular programming languages, to be packaged and deployed in the FaaS model. There are also open source solutions available, such as Apache OpenWhisk (*https://openwhisk.apache.org*) or Fn project (*https://fnproject.io*), that implement FaaS with Docker. In the following sections, we will focus on Knative and Kubernetes, as we have discussed throughout the book how Kubernetes provides a complete ecosystem for easing the migration of Java enterprise applications to the cloud native paradigm.

## Functions Deployment for Java Applications

Functions are a piece of code delivered according to the serverless model and are portable between different infrastructure configurations. The life cycle of a function is described in Figure 7-6 starting with code writing, as well as specification and metadata. The building phase automatically happens afterward, and the deployment publishes the function in the platform. This enables a mechanism of updates that will trigger a new build and a new publish when a new change is needed.

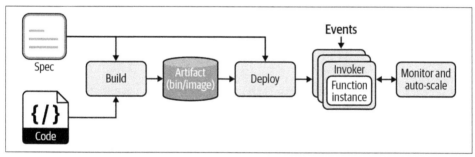

*Figure 7-6. Functions deployment model*

## Boson Function CLI (func)

Boson Function CLI (*https://oreil.ly/lKYKc*) is an open source CLI and framework that connects to Knative to provide FaaS capabilities to Kubernetes. With this tool, you can avoid writing Kubernetes manifests and building the container image yourself, as it will be done automatically:

```
$ func
...
Available Commands:
  build      Build a function project as a container image
  completion Generate completion scripts for bash, fish, and zsh
  create     Create a function project
  delete     Undeploy a function
  deploy     Deploy a function
  describe   Show details of a function
```

```
emit       Emit a CloudEvent to a function endpoint
help       Help about any command
list       List functions
run        Run the function locally
version    Show the version
...
```

 You can download the latest func CLI from the official website (*https://oreil.ly/d6oXo*) and configure it to your system.

Functions can be deployed to any Kubernetes cluster that has been configured to support serverless workloads, such as with Knative.

Currently, func CLI supports these programming languages and frameworks:

- Golang
- Node.js
- Python
- Quarkus
- Rust

Let's create a Quarkus function inside the coolstore namespace that you created in the previous sections. You can also find this function in this book's GitHub repository (*https://oreil.ly/M3yPE*).

To create a new Quarkus function, run this command specifying the -l option to select the language as follows:

```
$ func create -l quarkus quarkus-faas
```

You should get a similar output:

```
Project path: /home/bluesman/git/quarkus-faas
Function name: quarkus-faas
Runtime: quarkus
Trigger: http
```

This created a skeleton of a Maven project for Quarkus, with a POM file containing all dependencies needed:

```
$ tree
.
├── func.yaml    ❶
├── mvnw
├── mvnw.cmd
├── pom.xml      ❷
```

```
├── README.md
└── src
    ├── main
    │   ├── java
    │   │   └── functions
    │   │       ├── Function.java ❸
    │   │       ├── Input.java
    │   │       └── Output.java
    │   └── resources
    │       └── application.properties
    └── test
        └── java
            └── functions
                ├── FunctionTest.java
                └── NativeFunctionIT.java
8 directories, 11 files
```

❶    This is the file containing configuration information for your function project.

❷    The POM file for this Quarkus project.

❸    The Java class containing annotations and code to run the function.

Let's add some content for the func.yaml function's configuration file to transform your function into a runnable container image on Kubernetes:

```
name: quarkus-faas ❶
namespace: "coolstore" ❷
runtime: quarkus ❸
image: "docker.io/modernizingjavaappsbook/quarkus-faas:latest" ❹
imageDigest: ""
trigger: http ❺
builder: quay.io/boson/faas-quarkus-jvm-builder ❻
builderMap:
 default: quay.io/boson/faas-quarkus-jvm-builder
 jvm: quay.io/boson/faas-quarkus-jvm-builder
 native: quay.io/boson/faas-quarkus-native-builder
env: {} ❼
annotations: {} ❽
```

❶    Name of the function.

❷    The Kubernetes namespace where your function will be deployed.

❸    The language runtime for your function declared at creation time.

❹    This is the image name for your function after it has been built.

❺    The invocation event that triggers your function. For example, http for plain HTTP requests such as in this case, or event for CloudEvent-triggered functions.

❻ Specifies the buildpack builder image to use when building the function.

❼ Reference to any environment variables that will be available to your function at runtime.

❽ Annotations for the function to be used to tag items.

 func builds functions and transforms them in container images with Buildpack (*https://buildpacks.io*), a popular open source project used to build source code into a runnable application container image.

Let's review the POM file:

```xml
<?xml version="1.0"?>
<project xsi:schemaLocation="http://maven.apache.org/POM/4.0.0↳
  https://maven.apache.org/xsd/maven-4.0.0.xsd" ↳
xmlns="http://maven.apache.org/POM/4.0.0"↳
    xmlns:xsi="http://www.w3.org/2001/XMLSchema-instance">
  <modelVersion>4.0.0</modelVersion>
  <groupId>org.acme</groupId>
  <artifactId>function</artifactId>
  <version>1.0.0-SNAPSHOT</version>
  <properties>
    <compiler-plugin.version>3.8.1</compiler-plugin.version>
    <maven.compiler.parameters>true</maven.compiler.parameters>
    <maven.compiler.source>1.8</maven.compiler.source>
    <maven.compiler.target>1.8</maven.compiler.target>
    <project.build.sourceEncoding>UTF-8</project.build.sourceEncoding>
    <project.reporting.outputEncoding>UTF-8</project.reporting.outputEncoding>
    <quarkus-plugin.version>1.13.0.Final</quarkus-plugin.version>
    <quarkus.platform.artifact-id>quarkus-universe-bom</quarkus.platform.
     artifact-id>
    <quarkus.platform.group-id>io.quarkus</quarkus.platform.group-id>
    <quarkus.platform.version>1.13.0.Final</quarkus.platform.version> ❶
    <surefire-plugin.version>3.0.0-M5</surefire-plugin.version>
  </properties>
  <dependencyManagement>
    <dependencies>
      <dependency>
        <groupId>${quarkus.platform.group-id}</groupId>
        <artifactId>${quarkus.platform.artifact-id}</artifactId>
        <version>${quarkus.platform.version}</version>
        <type>pom</type>
        <scope>import</scope>
      </dependency>
    </dependencies>
  </dependencyManagement>
  <dependencies>
```

```
    <dependency>
      <groupId>io.quarkus</groupId>
      <artifactId>quarkus-funqy-knative-events</artifactId> ❷
    </dependency>
...
  </dependencies>
...
  <profiles>
    <profile> ❸
      <id>native</id>
      <activation>
        <property>
          <name>native</name>
        </property>
      </activation>
      <build>
        <plugins>
          <plugin>
            <artifactId>maven-failsafe-plugin</artifactId>
            <version>${surefire-plugin.version}</version>
            <executions>
              <execution>
                <goals>
                  <goal>integration-test</goal>
                  <goal>verify</goal>
                </goals>
                <configuration>
                  <systemPropertyVariables>
                    <native.image.path>${project.build.directory}/${project.build.
                      finalName}↳
-runner</native.image.path>
                    <java.util.logging.manager>org.jboss.logmanager.LogManager↳
</java.util.logging.manager>
                    <maven.home>${maven.home}</maven.home>
                  </systemPropertyVariables>
                </configuration>
              </execution>
            </executions>
          </plugin>
        </plugins>
      </build>
      <properties>
        <quarkus.package.type>native</quarkus.package.type>
      </properties>
    </profile>
  </profiles>
</project>
```

❶  Version of Quarkus

❷  Quarkus Funqy dependency, a Java API for FaaS environments

---

❸ Native profile for building Quarkus native applications

Quarkus Funqy (*https://oreil.ly/1CNPK*) is part of Quarkus's support for serverless workloads and aims to provide a portable Java API to write functions deployable to various FaaS environments, such as AWS Lambda, Azure Functions, Knative, and Knative Events (Cloud Events). Funqy is an abstraction that spans multiple different FaaS providers and protocols. It is optimized for small workloads and faster execution while providing a simple framework with no overhead.

Let's look at the source code of the Java function generated in the `src/main/java/functions/Function.java` path:

```
package functions;
import io.quarkus.funqy.Funq;
public class Function {
    @Funq ❶
    public Output function(Input input) {  ❷
        return new Output(input.getMessage());
    }
}
```

❶ To enable a function, you simply need to annotate your method with the `@Funq` annotation that comes from Quarkus Funqy API.

❷ Java classes can also be used as input and output. They must follow the JavaBean convention and have a default constructor. Here we are using `Input` and `Output` Beans.

Let's look at the source code of the `Input` JavaBean generated in the `src/main/java/functions/Input.java` path that will be used to represent input messages to the function:

```
package functions;

public class Input {
    private String message;

    public Input() {}
    public Input(String message) {

        this.message = message;
    }
    public String getMessage() {
        return message;
    }

    public void setMessage(String message) {
        this.message = message;
```

```
        }
    }
```

And let's have a look at the source code of the Output JavaBean generated in the src/main/java/functions/Ouput.java path:

```
package functions;

public class Output {
    private String message;

    public Output() {}

    public Output(String message) {
        this.message = message;
    }

    public String getMessage() {
        return message;
    }

    public void setMessage(String message) {
        this.message = message;
    }
}
```

We are now ready to build the function. By default, the Boson CLI will connect to the local Docker instance locally to create the container with buildpacks and then push to the container registry you declared in the func.yaml configuration file:

```
$ func build
```

 In future versions, Boson CLI will also delegate the building phase to Kubernetes via Tekton.

After a few minutes, you should get a similar output:

```
Function image built: docker.io/modernizingjavaappsbook/quarkus-faas:latest
```

After the function has been built, you can test it locally as a running container image before deploying it to Kubernetes:

```
$ func run
```

You should get an output similar to this:

```
exec java -Dquarkus.http.host=0.0.0.0 -Djava.util.logging.manager=org.jboss.
logmanager.LogManager -XX:+ExitOnOutOfMemoryError -cp . -jar /layers/dev.
boson.quarkus-jvm/app/app.jar
```

```
  __  ___  __  ____  __ __  __  ___  ____
 --/ _ \/ / / / _ | /  |/ / //_/ / / / _/
 -/ /_/ / /_/ / __ |/ /|_/ / ,< / /_/ /\ \
 --_____/_/ |_/_/ /_/_/|_|\____/___/
2021-06-25 16:51:24,023 INFO [io.quarkus] (main) function 1.0.0-SNAPSHOT on JVM
(powered by Quarkus 1.13.0.Final) started in 1.399s. Listening on:
http://0.0.0.0:8080
2021-06-25 16:51:24,027 INFO [io.quarkus] (main) Profile prod activated.
2021-06-25 16:51:24,028 INFO [io.quarkus] (main) Installed features: [cdi,
  funqy-knative-events]
```

In another terminal, verify the process is running:

```
$ docker ps | grep modernizingjavaappsbook/quarkus-faas:latest
cd1dd0ccc9b2  modernizingjavaappsbook/quarkus-faas:latest  "/cnb/process/web"
  3 minutes ago  Up 3 minutes  5005/tcp, 127.0.0.1:8080->8080/tcp
  musing_carson
```

Try to access it:

```
$ curl \
 -X POST \
 -H "Content-Type: application/json" \
 -d '{"message":"Hello FaaS!"}' \
http://localhost:8080
```

You should get an output similar to this:

```
{"message":"Hello FaaS!"}
```

Now let's deploy it to Kubernetes and let Knative use it as a scale-to-zero application.
When we invoke the function via HTTP, Knative will start it automatically, and it will
scale down to zero when not used:

```
$ func deploy
```

After a few seconds, you should see an output similar to this:

```
Deploying function to the cluster
  Function deployed at URL: http://quarkus-faas.coolstore.192.168.39.69.nip.io
```

Finally, start your Quarkus function on Kubernetes!

```
$ curl \
 -X POST \
 -H "Content-Type: application/json" \
 -d '{"message":"Hello FaaS on Kubernetes!"}' \
http://quarkus-faas.coolstore.192.168.39.69.nip.io
```

You should get an output similar to this:

```
{"message":"Hello FaaS on Kubernetes!"}
```

You can verify that a new pod has started in your Kubernetes cluster inside the `cool store` namespace:

```
kubectl get pods -n coolstore
NAME                                          READY  STATUS   RESTARTS  AGE
curl                                          1/1    Running  3         9d
quarkus-faas-00001-deployment-5b789c84b5-kc2jb 2/2   Running  0         80s
```

And, you should see that a new Knative Service has been created:

```
kubectl get ksvc quarkus-faas -n coolstore
NAME         URL                  LATESTCREATED     LATESTREADY        ...
quarkus-faas http://quarkus...nip.io quarkus-faas-00001 quarkus-faas-00001 ...
```

You can now see all the details of your newly deployed function with the following command:

```
kubectl describe ksvc quarkus-faas -n coolstore
```

You should get an output similar to this:

```
Name:        quarkus-faas
Namespace:   coolstore
Labels:      boson.dev/function=true
             boson.dev/runtime=quarkus
Annotations: serving.knative.dev/creator: minikube-user
             serving.knative.dev/lastModifier: minikube-user
API Version: serving.knative.dev/v1
Kind:        Service
Metadata:
 Creation Timestamp: 2021-06-25T17:14:12Z
 Generation:         1
....
Spec:
 Template:
   Metadata:
     Creation Timestamp: <nil>
   Spec:
     Container Concurrency: 0
     Containers:
       Env:
         Name:  BUILT
         Value: 20210625T171412
       Image:   docker.io/modernizingjavaappsbook/quarkus-faas@↵
sha256:a8b9cfc3d8e8f2e48533fc885c2e59f6ddd5faa9638fdf65772133cfa7e1ac40
       Name:    user-container
       Readiness Probe:
         Success Threshold: 1
         Tcp Socket:
           Port: 0
       Resources:
     Enable Service Links: false
     Timeout Seconds:      300
 Traffic:
```

```
     Latest Revision: true
     Percent:        100
  Status:
   Address:
    URL: http://quarkus-faas.coolstore.svc.cluster.local
   Conditions:
     Last Transition Time:       2021-06-25T17:14:22Z
     Status:                     True
     Type:                       ConfigurationsReady
     Last Transition Time:       2021-06-25T17:14:22Z
     Status:                     True
     Type:                       Ready
     Last Transition Time:       2021-06-25T17:14:22Z
     Status:                     True
     Type:                       RoutesReady
   Latest Created Revision Name: quarkus-faas-00001
   Latest Ready Revision Name:   quarkus-faas-00001
   Observed Generation:          1
   Traffic:
     Latest Revision: true
     Percent:        100
     Revision Name:   quarkus-faas-00001
   URL:                          http://quarkus-faas.coolstore.192.168.39.69.nip.io
  Events:
   Type    Reason   Age    From                Message
   ----    ------   ----   ----                -------
   Normal Created 4m15s service-controller Created Configuration "quarkus-faas"
   Normal Created 4m15s service-controller Created Route "quarkus-faas"
```

# Summary

In this chapter, we analyzed how Java developers can create modern applications following the serverless execution model. We outlined some of the most common use cases and architectures that Java developers are likely to work with today, and tomorrow. Edge computing, Internet of Things, data ingestion, and machine learning are all contexts where event-driven architectures are a natural choice, and where serverless and Java can play a strategic and supporting role. We discussed FaaS, which represents the latest evolution in software development, and how Kubernetes can automate the whole life cycle of applications deployed as decoupled, asynchronous, easy-to-parallelize processes called functions.

With this chapter, we complete this "Concise Cloud Native Guide for Developers." From microservices to functions, Java developers today have a complete set of frameworks, tools, and platforms such as Kubernetes that can help them modernize their architectures, innovate their solutions, and look ahead to solve the next challenges in today's IT context. This context is one that is ever more heterogeneous, ubiquitous, large scale, and cloud native.

To you I have given wings, on which you may fly aloft

Above the boundless sea and all the earth [...]

To all who care for them, even to those who are not yet born, you will be

Alike a theme of song, so long as Earth and Sun exist.

    —Theognis of Megara

# Index

## Symbols

microservices
    APIs and, 103
    authentication and, 53
    authorization and, 53
    Catalog Service, 12
        Spring Boot, 23-32
    debugging, 110
        port forwarding, 111
        Quarkus remote development, 112
        Telepresence, 113-115
    distributed systems and, 46
    frontend, 41-43
        dependencies, 42
        NPM, 42
        running, 42
    Gateway service, 12
        Vert.x, 33-41
    Inventory Quarkus, 64
    Inventory service, 12
        domain model, 17
    Kubernetes, 63, 64
    Kubernetes Services and Pods, 104
    Model layer, 13
    monolith interaction, 93
    Presentation layer, 13
    Quarkus, 13
    querying, 22
    versus monolithic style, 46
    WebUI service, 12
microservicilities, 51
migration
    6 Rs, 48
    application assessment, 86-88
    application portfolio, 57
    challenges, 98-99
    legacy protection, 92
        database separation, 94-95
        service to monolith interactions, 93
    refactoring, 95
        component models, 97
        MicroProfile, 96
        Quarkus, 97
        Spring, 98
    replatforming, 92
        database separation, 94-95
        service to monolith interactions, 93
Migration Toolkit for Applications (MTA),
    89-90
ML (machine learning), 46

serverless computing, 119-120
Model layer, 12
    microservices and, 13
modernization, 46
    6 Rs, 47
        Refactor, 50
        Rehost, 49
        Replatform, 50
        Repurchase, 49
        Retain, 48
        Retire, 49
    application assessment, 86-88
        controls, 88
        DiVA, 89
        inventory, 88
        MTA (Migration Toolkit for Applica-
            tions), 89-90
        Pathfinder, 88
    budget considerations, 86
    containers, 49, 50-56
        images, 51
    cost versus benefits, 92
    effort estimation, 87
    functionality assessment, 91-92
    in-house skills, 86
    Java release cycles, 47
    operations and, 46
    progress prediction, 87
    refactoring, 57
    risk assessment, 87
monitoring, Kubernetes-native development,
    105
monolith architectures, 45
    breaking down, 57
    database separation, 94-95
    integration logic, 99
    legacy systems, 86
    logical model, 91
    modernization, functionality assessment,
        91-92
    services, 93
    types, 91
monolithic versus microservices style, 46
MTA (Migration Toolkit for Applications),
    89-90
multicloud environment, 2

# N

Newman, Sam, 57

## About the Authors

**Markus Eisele** is the developer adoption program lead for Red Hat in EMEA. He has been working with Java EE servers from different vendors for more than 14 years and gives presentations on his favorite topics at international Java conferences. He is a Java Champion, former Java EE Expert Group member, and founder of Germany's number-one Java conference, JavaLand. He is excited to educate developers about how microservices architectures can integrate and complement existing platforms, as well as how to successfully build resilient applications with Java and containers. He is also the author of *Modern Java EE Design Patterns* (*https://oreil.ly/WFJmH*) and *Developing Reactive Microservices* (*https://oreil.ly/38mgZ*) (O'Reilly). You can follow more frequent updates on Twitter (*https://twitter.com/myfear*) and connect with him on LinkedIn (*https://linkedin.com/in/markuseisele*).

**Natale Vinto** is a software engineer with more than 10 years of expertise on IT and ICT technologies and a consolidated background on telecommunications and Linux operating systems. As a solution architect with a Java development background, he spent some years as EMEA specialist solution architect for OpenShift at Red Hat. Today, Natale is a developer advocate for OpenShift at Red Hat, helping people within communities and customers have success with their Kubernetes and cloud native strategy. You can follow more frequent updates on Twitter (*https://twitter.com/natale vinto*) and connect with him on LinkedIn (*https://linkedin.com/in/natalevinto*).

## Colophon

The animal on the cover of *Modernizing Enterprise Java* is the onager (*Equus hemionus*). Onagers are similar to many wild donkeys in appearance, but are slightly smaller with a paler coat and a light brown dorsal stripe. They're found from Mongolia to Saudi Arabia, inhabiting flat regions of the deserts and surrounding foothills. In these harsh environments, onagers' diets consist of scarce grasses, bushes, herbs, and foliage, but they must remain close to a site of open water.

Onagers are not easy to frighten and are curious by nature. This makes them especially susceptible to hunters, who seek their meat and hides. Starting in 1971, onagers became a protected species, but despite efforts to curb human predation, it's estimated that only 395 mature onagers remain in the wild. Many of the animals on O'Reilly covers are endangered; all of them are important to the world.

The cover illustration is by Karen Montgomery, based on a black-and-white engraving from *Brehms Tierleben*. The cover fonts are Gilroy Semibold and Guardian Sans. The text font is Adobe Minion Pro; the heading font is Adobe Myriad Condensed; and the code font is Dalton Maag's Ubuntu Mono.